MICHAEL PARKINSON
ON CRICKET

Also by Michael Parkinson

Michael Parkinson on Football
Michael Parkinson on Golf
Cricket Mad
Football Daft
Sporting Fever
Bats in the Pavilion
Best – An Intimate Biography
A–Z of Soccer (with Willis Hall)
The Woofits
Parkinson's Lore
The Best of Parkinson
Sporting Lives
Sporting Profiles
Pictorial History of Westerns
(with Clyde Jeavons)

About the Author

Michael Parkinson began his career as a journalist on the *Manchester Guardian*. He started writing about sport for the *Observer* and wrote a column for *The Sunday Times* for fifteen years. His legendary talk show *Parkinson* is currently back on the BBC with huge success. He also hosts *Parkinson's Sunday Supplement* on Radio Two and writes a regular column for the *Daily Telegraph*.

MICHAEL PARKINSON

ON CRICKET

Michael Parkinson

Illustrated by John Ireland

Hodder & Stoughton

A CIP catalogue record for this title is available
from the British Library

ISBN 0 340 82507 3

Typeset in 11/15 pt Sabon by
Rowland Phototypesetting Ltd,
Bury St Edmunds, Suffolk
Printed and bound in Great Britain by
Mackays of Chatham

Hodder and Stoughton
A division of Hodder Headline
338 Euston Road
London NW1 3BH

Contents

Contents

INTRODUCTION

It is commonly supposed Yorkshiremen were created to love and understand cricket, if they so chose. In my case it was compulsory. My father dedicated his life to ensuring I grew up playing and loving the game. I am glad he did. It is the most English of games, complex and mysterious as Stonehenge; an acquired taste like mushy peas. I was never told fairytales as a child. Instead, I heard of Larwood's action and Hobbs' perfection.

My father was a remarkable man with a marvellous facility to adorn an anecdote. He swore he managed to see Len Hutton's 364 at The Oval by convincing the gate attendant that he was dying of some incurable disease and his last wish was to see Len before he took leave of this earth. I never swallowed that one until once at a football match when the gates were closed I witnessed him convince a gateman that he was a journalist and I was his runner. I was seven at the time, and it was the very first occasion I watched a football match from a press box.

Apart from being a fairystory teller Dad was a quick bowler with an action copied from his great hero, Harold Larwood. He had a marvellous agility and sure pair of hands near the bat, and as a batsman he was a genuine number eleven who often didn't know whether he'd play left-handed or right-handed until he got to the crease; not that it made much difference.

Of all games, he loved cricket the most. The only time I ever saw him lost for words was when someone confessed they neither knew nor cared. Then he would shake his head sadly, baffled that a great part of his world – for cricket was surely that – could mean so little to any other sane human being.

In more ways than the obvious one this book would not have been possible without him. It is a collection of journalism spanning more than forty years. The articles were written for the moment and were not meant to last. I asked Roddy Bloomfield (my editor and friend for most of those forty years) why he thought they were worth repeating. He said they made him laugh.

That did it. That and because they stand as a testament to a man I loved more than any other.

LIKE FATHER,
LIKE SON

JOHN WILLIAM PARKINSON

I OFTEN wonder if my love of cricket would have been as deep and lasting had I been born in Biggleswade of a father who played tennis. As it was, from the very moment I was born and identified as being male, I was destined for a lifelong affair with cricket. I had no choice in the matter.

My father had decided to dedicate his life to providing Yorkshire County Cricket Club with a new opening bat. This was his duty. At the same time he was guaranteeing for himself a companion to spend a lifetime first playing cricket at his side and then sitting with him while they both contemplated the intricacies of the most mysterious and beautiful of games.

I could play forward and back before I could read and I knew how to bowl an off-break before I could do joined-up writing. My earliest memories of childhood are of sitting with my mother watching my father run in to bowl. He was slim with thick, wavy hair and good shoulders. He had a reputation as a fast bowler. There were not too many batsmen who fancied facing him.

How old was I? All I know is that when I first saw him play I was no taller than a Harrow bat and weighed less than the big brown teapot they brewed the tea in. I was eleven when I started playing league cricket with my father. He was captain of the local team and I played

under him for two years before moving up the road to Barnsley and the big time.

This was what decided him to give up the game in order that he might stand behind the bowler's arm coaching his protégé with an extraordinary repertoire of dramatic gestures.

Marcel Marceau had nothing on my old man. His most dramatic mimes occurred whenever I attempted a late cut. I had a great liking for the shot which my father regarded as being both frivolous and profane.

His initial display of displeasure was a sorrowful shake of the head. This could be augmented by placing his hand on his brow like a man with a severe headache. If I persisted with the shot he would hit his brow with the heel of his hand and stagger around in dramatic fashion like a man who has just been told that his wife has run off with the lodger.

Dad's love of the game was absolute, his appetite for it insatiable. The first time my parents took me to Stratford to see the place where our greatest writer was born, we lost Father. He disappeared in the crush.

I remember panicking but my mother remained unflappable. She approached a policeman and simply asked directions to the nearest cricket ground where we found Father sitting in a deckchair by the sightscreen.

In his younger days his favourite holiday was a week at Scarborough – which he reckoned had the best beach wicket in Britain – or Butlin's, not because he particularly cared for the idea of a holiday camp, but because of the sporting competitions. He used to enter the lot and normally came

home with a couple of trophies for snooker or running or the mixed wheelbarrow race. He entered everything and anything and owed much of his success to his ability to talk an opponent to death. I once heard an irate tennis opponent say to him, 'Doesn't tha' ever shut thi' gob?'

'Only when other people are talking,' said my old man, with a disarming smile.

When he finished playing he took up coaching, first the local youngsters and then his three grandchildren. They, like me, are left-handed batsmen. Not because God made them so, but because the old man's theory was that not many players like bowling at left-handers. His other theory, based on a lifetime's experience, was that fast bowlers are crazy, so he determined to make at least one of my sons a slow bowler. The consequence of this is that I once had the only ten-year-old googly bowler in the Western Hemisphere.

The old man's name was John William, and he hated John Willy. If anyone addressed him thus when he was playing in his prime, the red alert went up and the casualty ward at Barnsley Beckett Hospital could look forward to receiving visitors.

He's been dead for several cricket seasons now, but I still think about him because he was a special man and I was lucky to know him. He was a Yorkshireman, a miner, a humorist and a fast bowler. Not a bad combination.

I only hope they play cricket in heaven. If they don't he'll ask for a transfer.

January 1993

WHAT'S BRED IN THE BONE

WHEN I was born my paternal grandmother tried very hard to have me called Melbourne because MCC had just won a Test match there. Fortunately my mother, a southerner of great common sense, would have none of it. Not so my father who, being a Yorkshireman and therefore cricket mad, was torn between Herbert (Sutcliffe), Percy (Holmes) or Hedley (Verity). Mother settled for Michael and would not budge. That was the only concession my old man made during the next twenty years which he devoted to producing a son who would one day play for Yorkshire.

At eleven I was playing in the team he captained, a child among men, a pimple among muscles. But I received no quarter because the old man would not have it. Considering the atrocious wickets we played on and the psychotic bowlers we faced, that I survived that period intact was due to my own fleet-footedness and not, as my father used to insist, to the rumour that God protected prospective Yorkshire cricketers. He based this on the fact that He was born just outside Barnsley.

After every game came the post mortem, the old man dissecting every innings I played, advising, criticising, stuffing my young head with the game's folklore. There was nothing selfish in this. He would have done the same for any kid my age because he couldn't stand the game being played badly. Only once did he use my

tender years to his advantage. We were playing at a ground near Barnsley on a wicket which gave every impression of being prepared by a mechanical trench digger. We got our opponents out for about 40 and were in trouble at 24 for 7 when the old man joined me at the wicket. He came to me and said, 'Just keep your head down and leave the rest to me.'

He walked to the non-striker's end and immediately engaged in conversation with their fast bowler who had taken five wickets and put two of our players into the casualty ward. As the fast bowler walked back to his mark the old man walked with him.

'Long run for an off-spinner,' he said as they walked side by side.

'Wheer's tha' think tha's going?' said the fast bowler, stopping on his walk back.

'Wi' thee,' said the old man.

'Aye oop, umpire,' said the bowler. 'Can't tha' stop him?'

The umpire shook his head.

'Nowt in t'rules says he can't walk alongside thee, lad,' said the umpire.

At the end of his walk back the bowler turned and began his run to the wicket and the old man kept pace with him stride for stride. Halfway to the wicket the bowler stopped.

'Aye oop, umpire, can't tha' see what he's doing?' said the bowler to the umpire at square leg.

'Aye, he's running alongside thee, lad, but there's nowt to say he can't,' said the umpire.

The bowler, shadowed everywhere by my old man, completely lost his head and bowled three balls which nearly killed third slip. After the third he turned to my old man and addressed him in what I understood to be called 'pit language'. The old man listened for a while and then turned to the umpire and said, 'Did tha' hear that, Charlie?'

'I did that, John William,' said Charlie.

'Does tha' reckon it's fit language for a schoolboy to hear?'

'No,' said Charlie firmly.

'Then we're off and claiming maximum points,' said the old man and marched from the field, taking me with him.

As we walked off I pointed out that I had heard that kind of language – and worse – before, so why had he taken umbrage?

'Tactics,' he said.

He proved his case by defending his action to the League Committee and being awarded maximum points for a game we hadn't a hope of winning.

Soon after, I left his team to play for Barnsley in the Yorkshire League. But he followed, giving up playing to watch me, as I've mentioned before. When I batted he would stand by the sightscreen semaphoring his displeasure with a series of anguished body contortions. His most spectacular demonstrations always occurred whenever I tried a late cut and missed. He believed firmly with Maurice Leyland that you never late cut before June and even then only if the moon had turned to green

cheese. I once played this shot in a game at Barnsley and, having missed, looked towards the sightscreen where the old man was going through his customary paroxysm of displeasure. As I watched, the stumper approached me.

'Are tha' watching what I'm watching?' he asked. I nodded.

'I reckon he's having a bloody fit,' said the stumper. 'Does tha' know him?'

'Never met him before in my life,' I said.

Whenever I got near a fifty he couldn't bear to watch and always spent ten minutes in the gents' toilet until the crowd noise informed him that I was either on 50 or out. I went to one fifty by hitting the ball into that very same toilet where it was fielded by my old man, who came out holding the ball gingerly but looking like a man who has found a gold nugget.

I never told him I didn't want to play cricket for a living. I didn't dare. The truth dawned when I realised a life's ambition and joined the *Guardian* (*Manchester Guardian* as it then was). Delightedly I crossed the Pennines to tell my parents. Mother was really pleased. Father said, 'It's not like playing cricket for Yorkshire.'

Later, he centred all his ambitions on my eldest son. When he was about to be born I was living in Manchester but working in London. I had reached a perfectly normal and satisfactory arrangement with the welfare state whereby my firstborn would be delivered into the world in a Lancashire hospital. Near the expected date of the birth I received a phone call from my father.

'Well, it's done then,' he said.

'What is?' I asked.

'I've moved t'wife to a nursing home in Yorkshire,' he said.

'But why? Mary was perfectly happy in Manchester,' I said.

'Maybe, but we've not only her to think about. What about t'baby?' he said.

'What difference does that make?' I asked.

There was a long pause. He was obviously trying hard to control himself. 'Supposin' it's a boy,' he said.

'I very much hope it is,' I said.

'And if it's born in Lancashire what happens then?' he said.

'Tell me,' I said.

'*It can't play for Yorkshire at cricket, that's what!*' he yelled, his temper getting the better of him. 'Anyway, like I've told you, I've had them shifted. It's proper thing to do, lad.'

A month later my first child, a boy, was born in a Wakefield nursing home. His name is Andrew. He was a good cricketer but he didn't play for Yorkshire. 'Point is he could have if he wanted to,' said my father. And he died a happy man.

EARLY DAYS

MY MOTHER had not realised when she married my father that she was taking on the Yorkshire County Cricket Club as well.

The realisation first dawned on her honeymoon, which father persuaded her to take in London. The trip from Barnsley to London in those days was a glamorous one and my mother was overjoyed at his thoughtfulness.

What she didn't realise was that Yorkshire were playing Middlesex at Lord's and she spent three days behind the bowler's arm while her husband sat, as he always did at any cricket match, with a huge smile on his face as if he was the happiest man alive.

By the time I had arrived upon Yorkshire soil and was able to stand up and hold a cricket bat, my mother had become a fair all-rounder. She averaged over 20 on Scarborough beach and was a useful donkey-drop bowler. Her sister, Auntie Madge, was our wicket-keeper and there have been few better standing up using a coat. They were both coached by my father, who believed anyone born in Yorkshire, man or woman, had a duty to play cricket.

Indeed, as I grew up and started playing street cricket, I often picked Eunice Bradbury in my side. She was as pretty as a picture and slender as a cane, but she could throw a cricket ball through a brick wall.

We played cricket all the time. When I look back at

my youth it was one long cricket match interrupted now and then by totally unnecessary matters like learning algebra or conjugating Latin verbs.

The first floodlit cricket match did not take place in Australia. It took place in the mining village of Cudworth outside No. 10 Moorland Terrace where our street lamp became the wicket and we played under flickering gas light until they called us in.

When it was really dark you couldn't see the bowler as he ran up. This disadvantage to the batsman was evened out by the fact that the bowler's run-up meant he had one leg in the gutter and the other on the pavement. This accounted for the appearance in local cricket of certain bowlers whose run to the wicket gave every indication that they were wearing a surgical boot. I once batted for four nights scoring 1,027 not out, a record not likely to be beaten in my lifetime – although my mate Barry came near it once, scoring 1,010 before being run out in dubious circumstances when he left his crease to go to the toilet.

There was not a single person in our street games, not a boy or a girl, who didn't have the ambition to play for Yorkshire. It wasn't so much that you wanted to as it was expected of you. As soon as you were big enough you played league cricket. In those days there were no friendly fixtures in Yorkshire. The Leagues were the spawning grounds of Yorkshire cricket. They were trawled with a fine mesh and the county missed very little.

I learned a lot from my father, particularly about

the art of psychological warfare. He was an expert at allusion, creating uncertainty among his opponents. I remember one day when he introduced a new fast bowler the opposition had never seen before. After the first over their opening bat said to my father, 'By gum, John William, but your new lad's a bit quick.' And my father said, 'He is that. But tha' should have seen him before he got gassed.'

It was tough cricket, as far removed from the romantic image as could be imagined. Where there should have been blue hills in the distance we had muckstacks, instead of deckchairs there were hard wooden benches. The men who sat on them had not come to enjoy themselves. Their job in life was to make the players miserable, to give them some stick. We travelled to away games in a coal lorry and often arrived looking like a touring version of the Black and White Minstrels.

Youngsters, no matter how young, were given no quarter. It was assumed if you were picked to play in the League you could look after yourself. If you couldn't, then tough. I remember my father being worked over by a young fast bowler who, after hitting him several times, finally offered a smirky, fairly sarcastic 'Sorry'. Whereupon my old man said, 'Nay, don't apologise lad, it's my turn next.' And he was as good as his word.

While I was playing for Barnsley, I did once receive an invitation to go to the Yorkshire nets for a trial, but I wasn't good enough. Maurice Leyland was coaching and he took one look at my late cut and sorrowfully shook his head. They liked the guy I was opening with

at that time, Dickie Bird. He went on to play for York-shire and, of course, had a long and distinguished career as an umpire. In my last season at the club before I came south, another lad got the nod. He was Geoffrey Boycott.

Just before he died, my father told me that I had had a fortunate life being able to meet my heroes and write about sport. Then he said to me, 'But you know, lad, none of it is like playing cricket for Yorkshire, is it?' And I had to agree.

If you heard a noise when Yorkshire decided to change the rules concerning home-born players, it was my father turning over in his grave. And given that what I have just described of growing up in Yorkshire was an even stronger part of his heritage, it would be amazing if he hadn't moved.

But things are different now. Everything changes and if the club doesn't then it is doomed.

The fact is that even with the advent of overseas players, fathers will still take their pregnant wives to the county. It is part of the folklore of being Yorkshire. The White Rose will always mean something special in cricket whether worn by a man born in Barnsley or in Bangladesh – because it was once the most feared and respected emblem in all the cricketing world.

At least, that's what I think. But I'm dreading what the old man is going to say to me when next we meet. Not to mention Lord Hawke.

LIKE FATHER, LIKE SON

MAIDENHEAD and Bray Extras XI – which is a polite way of describing the third team – was at one time in danger of being overrun by Parkinsons. There were two of us in the team – myself and Andrew, then a fourteen year old – with two others, Nicholas (ten) and Michael (six), operating the scoreboard. Mrs Parkinson was often the sole spectator, and what is more, John William Parkinson, my old man and chieftain of the tribe, was constantly threatening a comeback as an umpire. If this had happened, he would have been an umpire with a unique outlook on the job.

For instance, he was the only umpire I knew who constantly offered advice to the bowlers. Thus every delivery was followed by a 'Pitch 'em up' or 'Blow him a bouncer' or 'Get thi' bloody hair cut'. Also, he was one of the few umpires of my experience who appealed along with the bowler. Many's the time he leapt in the air and joined with the bowler in an ear-shattering appeal for lbw, leaving the departing batsman with serious doubts about the supposed impartiality of the adjudicator.

Once he appealed for a catch behind the wicket and discovered to his chagrin, after his cry had echoed round the field, that his had been the only voice raised in anguish. As the fielders and a startled batsman regarded him with awe, he straightened his tie, cleared his throat and said, 'Not out, you silly old bugger.'

Maidenhead and Bray Extras XI, however, was spared the experience of having my old man as umpire. He delayed his comeback until the party to tour Australia at the time was announced. He lived in hope that they would send for him as baggage man or the like, or that they would consult him in matters of team selection.

He had had his team selected for some time. It was: D.B. Close (Somerset) captain, R. Illingworth (Leicestershire) vice-captain, G. Boycott (Yorkshire) deputy vice captain, B. Wood (Lancashire), J. Balderstone (Leicestershire), J.H. Wardle (Cambridgeshire), J. Laker (BBC TV Centre), F.S. Trueman (Batley Variety Club), plus the rest of the current Yorkshire side. He felt certain that this team would conquer the world.

However, all that is by the by and nothing whatsoever to do with the Maidenhead and Bray third team, except for the fact that, by playing in the same team as my son, I was reliving the time a million summers ago when I played in the same team as my old man.

In those days he was coming to the end of a career as a fast bowler of real pace and hostility, during which time he had achieved a reputation which made him as welcome on the playing fields of South Yorkshire as a family of moles. He captained the second team and collected around him a gang of raggy-arsed miners' sons which he turned into a cricket team – and a good one at that.

Under his critical gaze we learned the basics of the loveliest of games like play back, play forward and never hook or cut until the chrysanthemums have flowered.

He taught us the game's intricacies and mysteries, like lifting the seam on the ball with a thumbnail, maintaining its shine with Brylcreem, and the tactical virtue of the bouncer followed by the yorker. 'One to make his eyes water, the other to knock his pegs over,' he'd say.

He was a stickler for doing things properly, for people looking the part. He would not allow anyone in his team who was what he considered to be 'improperly dressed', which in his eyes would be someone wearing black socks or brown plimsolls. At this time there were a good number of youths in our team who didn't own the proper equipment – their parents either didn't care or couldn't afford it – but no one ever took the field in father's team unless he looked like a proper cricketer. He insisted on all of us going to the wicket correctly padded and protected. In those days it was commonplace to see a cricketer wearing one pad and no batting gloves, and a protector was something only wicketkeepers and pansies wore. Father would have none of it, and would even admonish youngsters on opposing teams who came to the wicket less than adequately protected.

If the youngster wearing one pad refused his advice to return to the pavilion and put the other pad on, he would take the ball and aim at the unprotected leg. He was still accurate enough to hit it and quick enough to make his victim wish he had taken his advice.

Eventually we grew up under his wing and became a team of young men. Then we broke up and went our

different ways, some into the first team, some to different clubs and higher leagues. As I have said, I went to Barnsley and the old man retired to come and watch me play, standing behind the bowler's arm wincing at my foolishness in cutting when the chrysanthemums were a long way from flowering.

I used to laugh with him and at him a lot, marking him down as a character and thinking he represented a generation and a lifestyle that was totally different from mine. He was, I reckoned, a man I'd never be.

Then when I started to play with my son I had the feeling that I was seeing a familiar landscape, the sense that I had been there before. When Andrew threw the new ball to the bowler on the bounce I said, 'Up, up, keep the bloody thing up,' and my father's voice came echoing down the years.

When he made a brilliant stop I grinned like an idiot and when he let the ball through his legs I felt like hitting him with the stump. In one game he had to go out and block for a couple of overs to save the game, and I told him how to play the off-spinner with bat and pad together, bat angled down and straight down the line.

I took up my position by the sightscreen playing every ball with him and damn me if he didn't walk down the track to the first ball and drive it through mid-on. It was not what I had told him to do, and I semaphored my displeasure. As I did so I saw the stumper looking at me in an odd way and having a word with my son. Does this sound familiar?

I knew what the wicket-keeper was saying to my son

because although times have changed and everyone in our team wears proper pads and protectors and no one plays in brown plimsolls, the fundamentals remain the same.

The fact is me and my old man are peas from the same pod, like father like son, and what I learned at his knee about the most beautiful of games is part of a heritage that I found myself passing on to my sons. I stood by that sightscreen and didn't care what the stumper was thinking. In that precious moment I was a man contented and fulfilled.

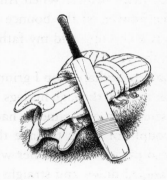

GRANDDAUGHTERS CHANGE
THE RULES

W HEN I heard we were to have our first grandchild I immediately made plans. The child would bat left-handed, bowl seam up and field in the gully just like his father, grandfather and great-grandfather before him.

There would have to be a ceremonial handing over of the cigarette card collection – Wills County Cricketers of 1928 and 1932, the John Player collection of soccer stars of the 1920s – plus the signed portrait of Dr W.G. Grace which now looks down on anyone using our ground-floor toilet. Most importantly, he would grow up living with the photograph of Herbert Sutcliffe, Len Hutton and Geoffrey Boycott taken in front of the pavilion at Headingley. It would hang in his nursery so that from the very earliest days he would know of his heritage and his destiny.

I decided that he would also inherit the baggy green cap of the Australian cricketer once worn by my dear friend Jack Fingleton, and the Australian cricket sweater given to me by the wondrous K.R. Miller.

I also found a brochure celebrating MCC winning the Ashes in Australia in 1928–29, which was sent to me by a cricket lover after I had written an article speculating on the best England cricket team of all time. The sepia faces stare at me through the spent years looking proud and confident, as well they might having just beaten the Aussies 4–1.

It would be difficult to pick a better team than that one containing Hammond (he averaged 112 in the Tests, scoring more than 900 runs), Sutcliffe, Hobbs, Hendren, Leyland, Phil Mead, George Geary, J.C. White, Harold Larwood, Maurice Tate and Ernest Tyldesley. Chapman was the captain, Jardine was sizing up Bradman and the wicket-keepers were George Duckworth and Les Ames.

The Australian team wasn't shabby either, with Bradman, Bill Woodfull, Alan Kippax, Archie Jackson, Clarrie Grimmett and Bill Ponsford in the side. Nearly 900,000 spectators watched the five Test matches. Those were the days, as my grandchild would be told when we visited the cricket together and watched the rain bounce off the covers and the grey clouds sweep in from deep fine leg.

I knew how to be a grandfather long before I became one, mainly by watching my own father with our three boys. By the time they were five they owned their own cricket bats and had been taught to bowl overarm. They were not much older when they were introduced to a hard ball and went to bed at night with lumps on their shins and stinging palms.

Before he took his 11-plus, Nicholas, the prospective grandchild's father, was proficient at the leg-break, could bowl a reasonable googly and was about to perfect the flipper when he fell victim to homework.

This greatly disappointed his grandfather, who believed that a real scholar was someone who mastered the mysteries of leg-spin bowling. He intended to prove the point with Nicholas but was finally thwarted in his

ambition by hormones, because when the child gave up homework it was because he had discovered girls.

I would tell his son – my grandchild – of his father's waste of a great and unique talent and try to persuade him not to do the same.

All these things, and more, were going through my mind as we awaited the big day. I found an old cricket bat which I intended to saw down to size as soon as his hands were large enough to grip the handle. I also searched out some golf clubs which I would adapt to his physique as soon as he was able to swing without falling over. After all, it would be something of an achievement if the lad opened for Yorkshire and England *and* played in the Ryder Cup.

I was making all these plans when a phone call came from Sydney, Australia, to tell us that our first grandchild had been born – a bouncing baby girl. I asked my son if he was certain the baby was female. He said there could be little doubt.

When I first saw Laura I thought she bore a remarkable resemblance to (the late) Colin Cowdrey, with her chubby cheeks and winsome smile. My wife said I was over-reacting. She might be right because on closer acquaintance I thought she could become that rarest of athletes, a good-looking shot-putter.

She is undeniably beautiful, but more than that she already eats her weight every day and, if she keeps it up, will not only be ready to win the shot, as well as the javelin and the discus, at the Manchester Olympics in 2012, but she will also be the first woman in Olympic

history to win a gold medal in a field event and simultaneously be on the front cover of *Vogue*.

It may be, of course, that the genetic inheritance is overwhelming, in which case she could well captain the England women's cricket team. I spent two months in Sydney looking for signs.

One day when I was trying to get her off to sleep by telling her how I used to play cricket with her uncle, Sir Geoffrey Boycott (it never fails with her grandmother), she gave me an old-fashioned look and stuck her forefinger in the air. I didn't take much notice until she did it again. The next day she had become pretty good at this and by the time we left Sydney was doing a near-perfect impression of her other uncle, Dickie Bird. Maybe she will be the first female to umpire a Test match. Maybe she'll grow up knowing the difference between a legbreak and a googly. Do you think she'll appreciate Fingo's cap and Nugget's sweater?

While all this was taking place we became grandparents for the second time. Emma has the serene charm and colouring of Uncle David Gower and hands and feet like Curtly Ambrose. After generations of producing males to play for Yorkshire we are now embarked on a ladies' cricket team.

The big question is, will the Parkinson Collection of Sporting Memorabilia, so carefully nurtured over the years, find a welcoming home with the new owners? Will grandfather be able to overcome all his prejudices about women and sport and leap the gender gap?

All I can say is that at my time of life I welcome the

challenge. It could be that I come to understand, as the philosopher wrote, 'the arrogance of age must submit to be taught by youth'. Provided that youth knows the difference between a leg-break and an off-cutter, I'll listen.

April 1994

MY FIRST GRANDSON

MY first grandson was born last week. Mother and child are well. That's the good news. The bad news is the child was born in Sydney. I have nothing against the city, indeed it is possibly my favourite place in all the world since they knocked down the Cuban Ballroom in Barnsley. What concerns me is the possibility of the child playing cricket for Australia.

I have taken what steps I can to prevent this happening. I have written to the ICC, the TCCB and the Yorkshire County Cricket Club informing them of the happy event and making it clear that not only does the child qualify as an England player because both his parents are English, but there are compassionate reasons to be considered, such as my state of mind and the fact that the child's great-grandfather – the immortal John William Parkinson – would turn over in his grave at the thought of his bloodline wearing a baggy green cap.

The early signs are that the parents are being sensible. The child is to be called James Michael (as in Laker and Atherton, I presume, though I may be wrong). I would have preferred a third name. I think cricketers with three initials have a distinct advantage when it comes to selection. James Michael Geoffrey would have done nicely. J.M.G. Parkinson has a certain resonance about it. What worried me was the possibility of the parents succumbing to their environment and calling the child Shane Craig.

I have ordered the first cricket bat. It will be a Gunn and Moore with a creamy blade like the one I bought James's dad. If he uses it like his father, the neighbours had better shutter their windows because for all my insistence that he played forward and back and learnt how to stay there all day, just like his Uncle Geoffrey, he decided at an early age that he preferred to give the ball a good thump.

He was a more willing pupil with the ball. I was turning him into a useful medium-pace seamer until his grandfather intervened and taught him how to bowl a leg-break. At the age of seven or eight we owned the youngest leggie in English cricket.

In those days I was working abroad a lot and my children's sporting education was taken over by my father. This explains how my three children became left-handed bats though they are right-handed persons. You will remember that my father hated bowling at left-handers and reckoned he wasn't the only one. Cricketers who have bowled at Sobers, Lara, Gower and a few others I could mention will support his belief that they made life difficult for bowlers.

His other theory was that fast bowling is a mug's game. He was one himself, therefore entitled to the opinion. He believed slow bowlers had the easiest life and in Nicholas found a pupil both willing and able.

When the child was ten or so and I had just returned from a long trip abroad, my father took me into the garden to show me how the children had improved at cricket in my absence. When it came to Nicholas's turn

to bowl he started with three decent leg-breaks which I spotted and patted and then one that skidded through and struck me on the pad.

'That's his top spinner and you're plumb lbw,' said my father, proudly.

'Nonsense. It hit a pebble,' I said, and stayed at the crease. My father smiled and whispered in his protégé's ear. Next ball, leg-break. Or so I thought. Instead it turned the other way, beat my forward defensive shot and bowled me. My father wore a smile that went right round his face and ended at his back collar stud.

'That was t'other one,' he declared.

'What on earth are you talking about?' I said and glared at my son. 'It was a fluke, wasn't it?' I said to him. He shook his head. 'No Dad, it was my "goggly",' he said.

Later on John Boorman, the film director, used the incident in the screenplay of a lovely film called *Hope and Glory* to symbolise the way some families use the sporting rather than Gregorian calendar to mark the passing of time.

For some time we had the youngest 'goggly' bowler in the world living in our house. Had he kept at it we would never have heard of Shane Warne. I have told him he must, as soon as possible, pass on his secrets to his offspring, our grandchild. The sooner James Michael is initiated into life's great mysteries – and leg-spin bowling is surely one of them – the better.

The secrets of cricket are jealously guarded and I want my grandson to be as fortunate as my hero, Keith Ross

Miller, who was taught the art of swing bowling by George Henry Pope, of Derbyshire and England. While I was sitting with Keith at Lord's he started reminiscing about playing on his favourite ground. 'It was here I learned how to bowl,' he said, nodding to the middle.

He told me that during the Victory Tests when he was playing for the Australia Services team, he was urged to bowl for the first time in his career because the team didn't have any quickies. He said he found it easy to run in and bowl fast but hadn't a clue how to swing or cut the ball. He sought expert advice from George Pope, who was playing for England.

He could not have chosen a better teacher. No one knew more about swinging a cricket ball or moving it off the seam than George Henry. After he had given Keith a masterclass on how to bowl the away swinger, the in-ducker and the leg-cutter, he said, 'I have left the most important lesson to the last. The thing you must never take the field without is this . . .' Whereupon he removed the cap from his head and pointed to a thick film of grease inside the rim. 'A bowler's best friend,' he said. 'I started wearing Brylcreem after that,' said Keith.

When I think of my grandson and his future, I hope to live long enough to see him making his debut for Yorkshire. James Michael Parkinson is the latest in a long line of sporting Parkinsons. He will want for nothing. His grandmother is arranging with the pro at Wentworth for a set of sawn-off golf clubs. I'm oiling his bat and the *Wisden*s are in his name. In my sporting calendar

he should be showing some promise as a cricketer by the time of the Sydney Olympics. When Brian Lara is forty he ought to be impressing them at the Yorkshire nets and by the time David Gower is sixty he will be wearing the White Rose on his cap.

When this happens I shall either be very old bones or in a box. All he needs to remember is that if he doesn't do as he is told, his grandad will haunt him for the rest of his life.

September 1995

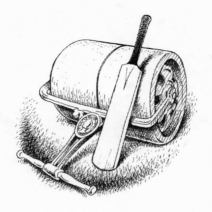

START OF PLAY

SCHOOLDAYS

I WAS talking to a chap the other day who was going on about the state of sport in our schools. He was making the point that at present the education system was doing for British sport what Dutch Elm disease did for our landscape.

In many schools, sports like cricket are not being taught any more; in some instances even if teachers want to teach a sport they can't because the playing fields have been sold off.

I started thinking if that had happened at my school I wouldn't have bothered turning up. I learned two skills at Barnsley Grammar School: how to smoke and how to play cricket. Both have proved lifelong afflictions.

In those days, before the educational theorists got to work, competitive sport was an important part of the school curriculum. It would have been easier for the headmaster to fire the Latin master than to get rid of our sports teacher. To win your colours at either cricket or soccer was to become a god.

I regarded academic subjects as being what we did in between the periods set aside for games. So did many of my friends, and, I suspect, one or two of our teachers.

Mr Swift, who taught cricket, soccer and maths, was renowned for gazing longingly towards the cricket field while teaching algebra on a summer's day and could easily be deflected from a lecture on geometry by the

proposition that if Pythagoras was alive and playing for Yorkshire he would bowl seam-up like Mr Coxon, not leg-breaks and chinamen like Mr Wardle.

Webb Swift and my father were the two men who most influenced the way I played and thought about cricket. There was no conflict in philosophy between them. They were both Yorkshiremen of a certain generation reared on the principles that batting was based on sound defence, bowling was a side-on art and cricket was a game best played in clean boots.

When I played my first net for Mr Swift I knew he was inspecting my father's handiwork. After ten minutes the nod of the head meant he was satisfied, as my father knew he would be. When people spoke of the Yorkshire system it was this continuum from family to teacher to club to country that was at the heart of it all. From our school playing field we could look down at the home of Barnsley Cricket Club. If Webb Swift did his job that would be the next step.

He was a stern teacher. He was a purist and a puritan about the game. As batsmen we were taught to play in the V. The bat must never move out of the perpendicular. Anything involving the bat moving out of a straight line was something you did later in life and only then if the ball was presented to you on a silver platter sitting up on a pile of cabbage.

If Mr Swift had a fault it was that he could never comprehend that now and again he would come across a child so swift of eye and reflex that he demanded licence within the framework of the coaching.

Such a one was Hector, a chubby and lumbering youth who was one of the best strikers of a cricket ball I have ever seen. He played like a young Colin Milburn with a long free swing of the bat and a natural timing. He murdered schoolboy bowling yet could never convince Webb he was anything other than a chancer and, what was worse, a heretic.

The conflict between them came to a head during the Masters versus Boys game when Webb bowled and Hector smashed him out of sight. Every time Hector came down the track and crashed him straight into the distant soccer pitch for six, Webb would shake his head sorrowfully and say, 'Nay, Hector lad, that's not the way to do it. Play it like this,' and he would demonstrate a dead bat forward defensive shot.

Then Webb would bowl it a bit quicker and shorter, pushing it through, and Hector would lay back and smack the ball past old-fashioned point. Webb would be almost weeping with frustration. 'Hector, Hector, how many times must I tell you, lad. When it's pitched there tha' does *this*,' and he would demonstrate lifting an imaginary bat above his head to enable the ball to pass safely through to the wicket-keeper.

And so it continued until Hector mistimed a hit and long-on caught him on the edge. He'd made 80 odd in no time and destroyed the bowling, particularly Webb's. But it didn't alter a thing. As Hector departed Webb Swift said to him, 'I warned you, Hector lad. That's what slogging gets you.'

He was aided in his search for perfection by the

groundsman, Mr Matthewman, who produced the best batting strip I have ever played on. Like most grounds-men, given the choice, he would have preferred that we looked at his masterpieces rather than trod on them.

He regarded cricketers as heathens who scarred his work. Our fast bowler was called Wilson and he de-veloped a pronounced drag in his delivery stride which ploughed a furrow you could plant turnips in. He turned up one day with a metal plate welded to his dragging toe cap in the manner of his great hero, F.S. Trueman. When he finished bowling it looked as if he had approached the wicket on a tractor. He was sent home before the groundsman saw the damage and murdered him with his reinforced footwear.

You had to play for the first team to get the chance to perform on John Matthewman's square. All other games were played on the out-field. When he had finished cutting and rolling the pitch he would take a razor blade and, on hands and knees, go in search of any errant weed or tumour. He sought perfection, and often achieved it. How many of us can say that? Only great artists, and he was one.

June 1990

THE DEBUT

THE first time you play cricket with the big boys is like your first love affair or the first taste of shandy on a sweaty day – something you will remember for the rest of your life. I can remember vividly to this day the first time I walked on to a cricket field with what my father always called 'proper' cricketers, which is to say men who didn't muck about on the field of play.

I can recall exactly the dressing-room smell of sweat and liniment and linseed oil, I can see the clothes hanging on the nails that served as pegs, and I remember my heroes one by one. The local hitter was Mr Roberts. He had a false leg and I often wondered what it looked like. Well, I found out that day they played me in the first team.

Mr Berry was our spin bowler and probably the most gifted player in the side. He bowled leg-breaks at about Underwood's pace and, when the mood took him, was unplayable. What I always wanted to know about him, however, was how he kept his sleeves up when he bowled. As someone who always contrived to look like an unmade bed after six overs in the field, I was envious of Mr Berry's ability to play through the longest and hottest day with not a ruffle in his outline nor a shirt-sleeve out of place. I watched him dress but never did find out the secret and dared not ask him in case he thought I was daft, or a wrong 'un, or both.

The quick bowlers were my old man and Mr Baker who had the longest run in local cricket. It was nothing for him to start his run from behind the sightscreen and on one ground, where there was a gate behind the bowler's arm, he actually started outside the field, bursting on to the scene like a runaway horse. Actually he had a gliding, smooth approach to the wicket and was a good-looking man with a handsome profile, and a liking for curved pipes and gentle conversation. By comparison his opening partner, my old man, was a volatile and explosive cricketer who expected, nay demanded, a wicket with every ball he bowled and woe betide any fielder with trembling fingers who stood between him and his ambition.

Our wicket-keeper was called Minty and he was a huge man with a bald head and a look of Telly Savalas. He wore the biggest protector I have ever seen, and he needed to because he stood up to every bowler no matter what the pace or the state of the wicket. His simple theory of wicket-keeping was that the job involved stopping a cricket ball with any part of the anatomy available. This accounted for his extra large protector and the bruises that covered him from head to foot after every game.

Those were a few of the people I shared the pavilion with on a hot August day when I made my debut with the local side. I was eleven or twelve at the time, a tin-tack in amongst the six-inch nails. I knew I wouldn't get a bat or a bowl and that I mustn't make a mistake in the field or else I'd get murdered by the old man when

I got home. On paper it seems a daunting prospect, but to me at that time it was the highlight of my life.

Two things happened in the game to convince me that I was right to want to be Len Hutton. The first was that someone swore on the field, using a word that in those days you would never use in front of eleven-year-old innocents. I looked quickly at my old man to see his reaction, but he just looked at me and winked, and I knew at that moment that I had been accepted into the brotherhood of cricketers and was not an impostor.

But the most marvellous moment came when I made a catch. It was a straightforward effort but I held it, and I knew they'd have to put my name in the score book and there would be proof of my existence. Moreover, there was a chance I might get a mention in the local paper, but it didn't happen. Mind you, I made up for the lack of publicity much later when I was working as a reporter on the local paper and also playing cricket every weekend. Then I wrote my own reports and became the best publicised player in South Yorkshire. Headlines like 'PARKINSON AGAIN' or 'ANOTHER PARKINSON TRIUMPH' were a commonplace in our local paper and even in the lean times the readers were guaranteed a 'PARKINSON FAILS' headline every now and again just to keep the name fresh in their minds.

All these memories came drifting deliciously back when my then nine year old was asked to make his debut with the local club. The other two were already veterans, having been blooded young, but the little one I was holding back on the advice of his Uncle Geoff,

who had been working on the forward defensive stroke, and Uncle Illy, who had been showing how to get side-on in the delivery stride.

We knew of his selection the day before the game but didn't dare break the news to him until the next morning in order for him to sleep in untroubled peace. Otherwise the only way we could have persuaded him to have closed his eyes was by giving him a bottle of sleeping tablets and half a bottle of scotch. He took the field looking like an advert for soap powder, and a quick check around the field revealed that the only other participants smaller than him were the stumps.

He was hidden by the captain (who happened to be his elder brother acting on my instructions) in all the places where you don't expect a cricket ball to go, whereupon, inevitably, the opposition hit the ball to all those places where you don't expect a cricket ball to go. Still, he fielded well and earned my particular admiration for sensibly going the other way to a fierce top edge that would have given Derek Randall trouble.

But his big moment came when he had to come in at number ten to play out the last over. The opposition kindly looped gentle spin at him whereby he nearly decapitated short leg with a sharp pull off the middle of his bat. He came off flushed as a drunken sailor with three not out, and I immediately informed Alec (Bedser) of his availability. That was on a Monday. On Friday before he went to school I saw him looking at the sports pages in the local paper, and I knew what he was seeking. He looked in vain. I couldn't tell him what I knew, that you don't need a yellowed cutting to remind you of your first game with proper cricketers. It is burned in your mind forever.

BROTHERLY LOVE

I USED to play cricket with a man called Billy Hopkinson who made John McEnroe look like the best
behaved athlete in the world. Whenever he was given out
lbw his team-mates would evacuate the dressing-room,
taking all their gear with them, before Billy returned to
vent his rage on whatever he could lay his hands on.
The main sufferers were the unfortunate batsmen who
were at the crease immediately after Billy was given
out.

All they could do was stand and watch as their gear
came through the dressing-room window to be followed
by Billy's gear, the wooden benches, the matting carpet
and, on very bad days, the large brown teapot that the
tea ladies borrowed from the church hall and which was
only used for funerals and cricket matches.

As befitted a world-class tantrum-thrower, in the field
Billy Hopkinson could produce an outburst at the cor-
rect tactical time. He was the best ooer and aaher I ever
played with and also the best running commentator.

On arriving at the wicket the new batsman would
find Billy staring thoughtfully at a spot just short of a
length. 'Looks nasty to me that does,' he'd say, sometimes going down on his hands and knees to calculate
the size of an imaginary ridge.

'I've never fancied this wicket since our Albert got
his nose broke. Made a right mess it did. You could

hear the crack a mile away. Off a slow bowler, too,' he would say, while the batsman tried to look cool.

From that point on the batsman's survival depended on his ability to concentrate on his game while being subjected to a barrage of propaganda from Billy at first slip. Any ball that went past the bat would bring an anguished 'ooooh' or 'aaaah' from Billy. It didn't matter if it was a yard outside the off stump, Billy reacted as if it had passed through the wickets.

Not surprisingly, Billy wasn't the most popular cricketer in the district. There were many players who disliked being bowled out while in the middle of an argument with Billy about whether or not the previous ball had shaved the wickets.

One player dismissed in such a manner decided on swift justice. Instead of returning to the pavilion he set off after Billy waving his bat like a club. But Billy was soon three fields away and wisely he took no further part in the game, spending the afternoon at home and sending his missus down to the ground for his kit.

I only saw him beaten at his own game once and that was by a dark, squat little man who answered everything Billy said about him with a tiny smile, a neat bow of the head and a 'thank you very much'. Finally, Billy could endure it no longer. At the end of the over he confronted the batsman.

'Aye oop, mister. I've been talking to thee all afternoon and tha's said nowt. What's up?'

The batsman looked at him, smiled, bowed and said, 'Thank you very much.'

Billy turned in despair to the other batsman. 'What the bloody hell's up wi' thi' mate?' he demanded.

'Didn't tha' know, Billy? He doesn't speak English. He's Polish,' the batsman said.

'Polish!' said Billy. 'Polish! What's a bloody Polisher doing playing cricket?'

He was silent for the rest of the afternoon, only occasionally muttering the odd obscenity about foreigners. It never occurred to him that there was something very odd about a Pole who spoke no English and yet played cricket well. He was too busy fuming to consider that he might have been conned by a superior foe.

None of us dared put the point to him and indeed we were glad we hadn't for otherwise we would have missed those marvellous moments in subsequent matches when, after giving a new batsman the ritual spiel, he would look at him and say, 'I suppose tha' speaks English, lad?'

Normally his tantrums were designed to win a cricket match but once he lost one with a display of temperament which was spectacular even by his own high standards.

An occasional member of the team was Billy's brother, the aforesaid Albert who was reputed to have had his nose broken by a slow bowler. Whatever brotherly love they might have had for one another they kept well hidden on the cricket field. Billy believed Albert was useless and Albert's opinion of Billy was unrepeatable. The more tense the game, the more bitter became the feeling between them.

Their loathing of one another boiled over in one game when Albert was bowling the final over against the last two batsmen of the opposing side who wanted four to win. The very last ball of the game was struck by the number eleven straight to brother Billy who dropped the catch. Albert stood, hands on hips, glowering at his errant brother.

'You great twerp,' he bellowed.

Billy, by now purple with embarrassment at having dropped the catch and enraged by his brother, shouted back, 'Tha' don't deserve wickets bowling bloody long 'ops like that.'

'Don't make excuses. I could have copped that in mi' gob. Tha' couldn't catch pneumonia,' said Albert.

This proved too much for Billy. Picking up the ball he advanced on his brother. 'If tha' so good at catching let's see thi' stop this one,' he said. He was about four yards from Albert when he threw the ball with all his considerable power. Wisely, Albert ducked. The ball went for four overthrows and we had lost the match.

Billy and Albert were still arguing as we went back to the dressing-rooms. Later they went behind the pavilion for a fight and were still at it when we left the ground. They both retired soon after that and went to barrack Yorkshire, sitting at opposite ends of Bramall Lane.

Some years later I was reminded of Billy when I was playing for Barnsley against a team that contained a character renowned for his tantrums and his gamesmanship. He was a quick bowler and particularly

rough on young players. He was bowling against us in one match and doing well both as a talker and a bowler until our number five batsman came to the wicket.

He was a young spindly lad with National Health spectacles and a bat that seemed several sizes too large for him. As he took guard the fast bowler commenced the treatment. 'Sending in short-sighted dwarfs to play us now. Must be short of players,' he shouted to the wicket-keeper. 'Looks like he's lost his mam,' replied the keeper.

All this was by way of introducing the lad to the joys of playing with the men. The bowler winked at his colleague and marched back to the end of his run-up, quite convinced that this was a doddle. His first ball was just short and outside the off stump whereupon the batsman played the most beautiful back-foot shot between the bowler and mid-off. It was classic in execution, the left elbow as high and pointed as a church steeple, the shot of a class batsman.

The ball whistled past the bowler and rattled the sightscreen. The bowler gave me a wry smile.

'What's his name?' he asked.

'Boycott. Geoffrey Boycott,' I replied.

THE DREAMER

On the general question of cricketers and their dress, I must say that if asked to nominate the most elegantly attired player of my acquaintance I would have to hark back to the time I played with the unfortunate Rowbotham.

My best friend at the time was a dreamer called Barry who believed he was the reincarnation of L.C.H. Palairet. He had a picture of Palairet leaning nonchalantly on his bat after he and one Herbert Hewett had whacked the Yorkshire attack for 316 runs playing for Somerset in 1892. What Lionel Charles Hamilton Palairet (Repton and Oxford) possessed to attract a lad in a Yorkshire pit village who never saw him play was style. He had the reputation of being one of the most graceful stroke-makers of all time, and, if you looked at the photograph, he was obviously a man who had his cricket gear made in Savile Row.

Barry persuaded his mother to make him a couple of long-sleeved silk shirts out of an old parachute and spent a fortune on a pair of creamy flannels and buckskin boots. He hitched his trousers with a coloured tie and wore a cravat.

All this would have been laudable in another part of Britain, but in the Barnsley and District Cricket League he was a provocative figure. It wasn't just the manner of his dress but his attitude which got up the

opposition's nose. In the imagined accent of his hero and using what he assumed to be the vocabulary of someone educated at Repton and Oxford, he would shout, 'Spiffing shot,' to his partner, or indicate a run by saying, 'Just the jolly old one I think, old fruit.'

Having learned that his hero played soccer for the Corinthians, Barry joined the local soccer club and again flaunted his fashion sense by wearing his shirt outside his shorts in the manner of the great amateurs. His fantasy was a glorious one but doomed. The ferocious manner in which we conducted our sporting contests in Barnsley in those days made no allowances for the whims of dreamers. Barry was like a dandy in a slaughterhouse. What is more, once the novelty had worn off, his posturing became an annoyance to his team-mates. Being his best friend, I was aware of what he was doing and found it amusing and charming. Others, who were not allowed into his secret world and who were faced with a lunatic who spoke with a funny accent and thought he was someone else, took a different view.

The end came when he played a cover drive ('a Lionel' he called it) and was checking the final position against his picture of Palairet when he became aware that his partner, who happened to be our captain, had run two and was coming back for a third. Whereupon Barry held up his hand and said, 'Whoa, Skipper.' The skipper shouted, 'I'll give you "Whoa", you great pillock.' Startled from his reverie, my friend set off on a forlorn and fruitless journey to the other end, where he was given run out by an umpire who must have been persuaded in his judgement by the fact that our captain appealed loudest of all. This was the last time the name of L.C.H. Palairet was heard in our neck of the woods – except for once more. In the coming soccer season Barry was sent off for brawling with a centre-half who took exception to his Corinthian garb and made coarse statements about his manhood. When asked by the referee for his name, Barry replied, 'Palairet. Lionel Charles Hamilton Palairet. Repton, Oxford, Somerset, England and Corinthian Casuals.'

The last time I saw Barry he told me he was into motorsport and had taken part in a race from Lancashire to France. For reasons I couldn't quite make out he raced dressed as Field Marshal Rommel and had an interesting encounter in Stoke-on-Trent when his car broke down and he went into a local fish-and-chip shop to enquire about the location of the nearest garage. Apart from one or two curious looks he was treated with great respect by the customers, who acted as if it was a perfectly normal occurrence for a member of the German High Command to walk into their chip shop.

They probably sussed he was a Corinthian Casuals player in disguise in secret talks with Stoke City.

July 1993

WEEPING FOR VINTAGE WILLOW

I HAVE measured out my life in cricket bats. Curiously enough the first I owned was a two-face one made from a neighbour's fence. It didn't have a sweet spot. I don't think they were invented in those days. It was as rigid and dead as a plank of wood, which is what it was.

If you made contact with a hard ball it sent shock waves through your body. You got pins and needles in the arms and your teeth rattled. It was a crude prototype of the new design to be set before the MCC for approval.

It was rejected by the players of the Barnsley and District Backyard League as soon as we found an alternative. This was provided by an evacuee from London who brought with him a Patsy Hendren Autograph his dad had provided as soon as he discovered his son was being shipped to Yorkshire.

It was brown with age and linseed oil and half the blade had been sawn off to transform it into a junior bat. It was the only bat I played with which had a handle as long as the blade. Looking back it was also the only bat I can recall from my Yorkshire childhood that was not signed by Len Hutton.

No matter, the Patsy did us well. Our wicket was on a strip of land next to the chip shop and ideally placed to ambush the drunks as they lurched home from the

boozer. Invariably they would stop to watch our game and, without exception, demand a bowl. We would bet them threepence that they couldn't bowl out one of us in ten minutes and we rarely lost. The first five minutes would be fairly good-natured, but then the thought of losing to a snotty-nosed kid with half a bat in his hand would accelerate their ambition. When this happened it helped to be able to play the bouncer, not to mention the beamer.

It taught us a lot about survival and even more about the wondrous effect ten pints of Barnsley Bitter can have on the human imagination. When they arrived at our game they were colliers with a bag of chips, just this side of legless. But as soon as they removed their coats and had the ball in their hands you could tell who they dreamed about. Not surprisingly most bowling actions resembled either Alec Coxon or Johnny Wardle, who were then Yorkshire's two best bowlers.

Coxon ran to the wicket with his right arm jerking up and down rather like a man blowing up a tyre with a hand pump. Wardle sidled to the wicket giving none of his intentions away. He was like a man lobbing a bomb into a room. I always thought he ought to be wearing a black cloak and mask.

A couple of our customers modelled their actions on the Kent and England bowler D.V.P. Wright. This is how I became acquainted with Mr Wright's action some time before I saw him bowl. The first time I was convinced that the bowler was having a fit. It was only when I saw Mr Wright play that I realised it had been

a fair imitation. It is difficult to describe his action, which was long and bounding and so packed with physical curlicues that you would not have been surprised had he finished off with a cartwheel.

In the main our opponents were easy pickings because their ambition exceeded their ability. The only man we feared was our local fast bowler, Mr Baker, who had the longest run I have ever seen. Had he measured it out on our pitch it would have taken him across the road and halfway down our street.

His approach was smooth until halfway to the wicket, when he would execute an extraordinary movement rather like a man doing a rumba. You half expected him to arrive at the crease with Carmen Miranda on his arm. However, it didn't do to mock Mr Baker because, unlike most of our customers, he knew how to bowl and, what is more, generally hit what he was aiming at.

I was just into my teens when I graduated from the strip by the chip shop into our local team. By this time I owned a proper bat. It had a Len Hutton autograph and a short handle and its purchase was not so much a business transaction as an initiation ceremony into manhood.

We bought it from the sports department at the local Co-op for £3 10s. The blade was creamy and it had a wide straight grain. I loved that bat more than any other I have possessed and it lasted from pubescence to the start of National Service. I cleaned it with a razor blade and protected it with linseed oil.

When it chipped and splintered at the edges I had

it bound with string, and when there was more string showing than wood, I had a re-blade. I took it to my bedroom at night and practised forward defensive shots. I tried to copy my great hero Len Hutton, whose photograph was stuck on the inside of the wardrobe door. Aware, even in those innocent days, that someone might think this strange I glued a picture of Alice Faye next to Len.

I was only once unfaithful to my bat. That was when I was seduced by a flash number owned by Mr Stewardson, our big hitter. I was a nudger and a deflector and I always envied the way that Mr Stewardson could strike a cricket ball.

I had never seen a bat like his. The blade was covered by dark brown hide kept in place by tacks up the back of the bat. It had a long handle and seemed to weigh a ton. Mr Stewardson used it like a club and when he connected the ball would threaten distant parishes. It was unlike any bat I have seen. There was something strange and mystical about it. I think that when he finished with it he threw it into a lake near Camelot.

I wanted a bat like it very badly and one day asked Mr Stewardson where I might buy one. He said I couldn't because there wasn't another bat like it in the world. 'Does tha' want to know its secret?' he whispered. I nodded. He looked around to see that no one was listening and then said, conspiratorially, 'It's what the bat's covered in that meks t'ball go a long way. Does tha' know what it is?' I shook my head. He drew me close to his side and whispered, 'Kangaroo skin.'

I went to our sports shop but the man said someone was pulling my leg. I asked Mr Roberts, our other big hitter, if he had kangaroo skin on his bat. He said he didn't but confessed that the secret of his powerful hitting was that he used a ten-springer. I went back to the sports shop to order one. The man said he didn't have one in stock but he could sell me a left-handed cricket bat.

I dare not accuse Mr Roberts of pulling my leg. That would have been insensitive as he was one short of a pair in the leg department; not that he ever made any concession to his impediment. Indeed he used it to his advantage. He never bothered to wear a pad on his tin leg so that when struck upon it there would be a noise like a bell chiming. If the bowler dare to shout 'Ow's that?' the batsman would smile at him sweetly and say, 'One of clock and all's well.'

When next I changed my bat it was for a Gunn and Moore. This saw me through National Service and its cousins through the remainder of my career as a serious cricketer. The change to something more frivolous occurred when I started playing for various showbiz teams. By this time I had been reduced to accepting hand-outs from friends.

It therefore came to pass that using the same bat Geoffrey Boycott had scored 2,000 runs with – and by the look of it all off the middle – I top-edged an underarm delivery from Barbara Windsor and was caught by Sue Lawley. Most shaming of all was when I went to the wicket carrying a bat presented to me by that most

elegant and gifted of Australian players, Greg Chappell.
He had used it to score a century against England. He
signed it on the back and gave it to me to use in a charity
raffle. I decided that before I let it go I would try it out,
to see if it worked for me like it had for Greg. I dressed
for the occasion: clean whites, spotless boots, buckskin
pads (whatever happened to buckskin pads?). I took
guard making sure the wicket-keeper saw the autograph
on the back of the blade.

It was a showbiz game, but not in my head. I was at
Lord's opening for England and Michael Holding was
ghosting in towards me. The ball came through the air,
red and gleaming. I saw it all the way. I took the toe to
the line, swung my magic bat and hit a large and ripe
salad tomato. Everyone thought it was hilarious. None
of them knew the sacrilege that had been committed.

Nowadays I don't own a cricket bat. Instead I look
with incredulity at the various shapes and sizes. I picked
up one owned by my eldest son and I swear the handle
was as far round as a drain pipe. They cost more than
a hundred quid. You could have bought our field for
that, plus the chip shop. The game is overwhelmed by
technology with scoops and sweet spots and names like
Jumbo and Powerdrive.

What seems to have been forgotten is that a cricket
bat should be beautiful as well as practical, better
designed as a baton than a cudgel. Recently I played in
a game with a man who had a Patsy Hendren bat. It
was the colour of old furniture and glowed with care.
It was the brother to the one we used to play with all

those years ago. When it struck the ball I swear it made a noise like a bass gong. It was the sort of bat you could have a conversation about, and we did. It had belonged to the batsman's father and was a family heirloom used only on special occasions.

It was a tribute to a craftsman's art, not like so much today, a product of commercial gimmickry.

March 1991

START OF THE SEASON

O UR cricket season started under winter skies with arctic winds. It would not have been a surprise to have come across a polar bear in the car park or witnessed the heavy roller being pulled by a team of huskies.

Given the conditions the perfect team would have been: Captain Scott, Franz Klammer, David Vine, Eskimo Nell, Magnus Magnusson, Sonja Henie, Jean Claude Killy, Nanook of the North, Roald Amundsen and Torvill and Dean. Twelfth man: Captain Oates.

As a joke, one of our batsmen stopped the bowler from the river end in his delivery stride and complained to the umpire of an iceberg moving behind the bowler's arm. Our umpire could normally see the funny side of things but on this occasion was not amused, having lost the will to live despite the fact that he was wearing three pairs of interlocking combinations, a balaclava, a scarf and a polo-neck sweater.

One of the few consolations of growing older is that you can spend such days in the warmth of the bar rather than having to brave it out in the middle. I used to hate the start of the new season. It always seemed to take us to Bramall Lane against Sheffield or Headingley to play Leeds. Neither were idyllic, even in midsummer with the roses blooming. On an early spring day in Yorkshire, with your fingers like icicles and the face leaking from

every orifice, they were severe tests of character and determination.

In the days when I played for Barnsley, Mr George Henry Pope used to preside over Bramall Lane. He was professional and groundsman and under both guises delighted in demonstrating to young cricketers who thought they knew a thing or two the intricate art of swing and seam bowling.

He left little to chance. As groundsman, he made sure there was enough grass on the wicket to take the seam; as a professional of great and deserved reputation he felt free to give his comments and predictions on events. Thus, within earshot of the dressing-room, he would opine that the opposition would be lucky to make 50 and he would most certainly be on a collection.

I suppose I was sixteen or seventeen when I first played against Sheffield and Mr Pope. It was the first game of the season. It was gloomy and cold with fat, dark clouds sitting on top of the soccer stand.

It wasn't the loveliest ground in the world, but it might have been the most intimidating. In those days the cricket club shared the ground with Sheffield United Football Club and behind Mr Pope, as he ran in to bowl, was the dark and mysterious emptiness of the soccer stand. What it told you as you scanned the terraces from the middle was that this was a ground where serious business took place. If you came here to enjoy yourself, forget it.

In those days I opened with Dickie Bird and the only consolation was that if you thought I was nervous, then

you should have seen my partner. Mr Bird was a fine player but possessed of the nervous disposition of a squirrel. He is the only man I know who used to bite his fingernails through his batting gloves. He would turn up for the start of a season with a brand new pair of gloves and after three games he wouldn't have a finger-top left on them.

His other peculiarity was a desire to give all his gear away if ever he had a bad trot. He was cured of this when he did it once too often and his team-mates – who had hitherto always returned his gear when asked – made him buy it back.

I am certain Mr Bird was my partner that day at Bramall Lane when we walked out to take part in Mr Pope's masterclass. I remember we were bowled out for under 50, that Mr Pope took eight wickets and that he made the ball do everything except sit up and sing *The Rose of Tralee.*

I faced him for about eight overs and I don't recall ever getting the bat near the ball. He swung it both ways, seamed it and cut it about. He made it hum through the air and dance from the wicket.

All of it was accompanied by his relentless, non-stop commentary, thus: 'Oh, a little leg-cutter there I think. Went a bit did that. Possibly too much.' Or: 'Nice out-swinger, George. Too good for the opposition perhaps.'

His most intimate asides were directed at the umpire. The relationship had already been established before a ball had been bowled. As George handed his sweater to the official he would say: 'Good afternoon Mr Umpire.

How nice to see you again. And how are the prize marrows this year?' The umpire would be flattered that the great man had remembered his vegetables and would beam benignly.

'And the wife and two daughters?' George would enquire. By this time the relationship was such that the umpire was certain that George Henry Pope was a long lost relative. George was much too subtle to take immediate advantage. The first time he hit your pads he would give a long look, stifle an appeal and say to the umpire: 'A little too high perhaps.'

But the next time it would be 'Owzat!' at full volume with the umpire eager to oblige. I played against him three times and once I hit him for a boundary. I played him through mid-wicket for four. That was nearly forty years ago and I was so proud I can still remember what it sounded like as it came off the bat. I also recall that next ball he knocked my off peg out of the ground.

The first time I opened the season at Headingley against Leeds is also engraved deep on my memory, not to say etched on my soul. I never liked Headingley. I still don't. It lacks character and feels like it doesn't belong. It doesn't belong to the Yorkshire County Cricket Club, which is probably part of the trouble. But I think the real problem was that whenever I played there it always seemed to be 250 for 1 with Leeds batting and Dickie Bird and me worrying about padding up and going out to face the likes of the young Fred Trueman.

The first time I played at Headingley there was one

spectator and he sat in lonely splendour while Billy Sutcliffe and the Australian rugby league international Arthur Clues smashed a century apiece against us.

I didn't count, but it seemed to me as if about 170 of their 200 runs went past me at cover point. A good many ended at the feet of the solitary spectator, who would watch me in critical silence as I ran the fifty yards to retrieve the ball.

I decided to appeal to his better nature, saying, 'You might throw the ball back to save me running down here all the time.' He looked at me quizzically. 'Nay, lad,' he said. 'Tha' misunderstands. I've come here to watch *thee* work not to do any missen.'

What cricketers realise is that no matter how horrendous the first game of the season might be in terms of weather and lack of form, it is nothing compared to the awful pain that tortures the body next morning. The stretching and exercising of joints and muscles which have been dormant throughout the winter promotes an awful pain and stiffness.

I do not exaggerate when I say that on more than one occasion I have been rolled from my bed the morning after the first game. I found that if the wife could propel me from the marital couch I would make it on my hands and knees to the bathroom where, by using the towel rail and the edge of the wash basin, I could raise myself to a standing position. I could shave only by lowering my head to my hand because I couldn't raise my arm to my chin.

Going to work was a problem. For a day or two after

the first game I could only walk if I did my famous imitation of Groucho Marx. I remember one occasion – when I had also suffered a smack on the bridge of the nose during the first game, which left me with two splendid black eyes – that when I grouchoed on to the train the next morning, a middle-aged woman gave me a pitying look and offered her seat. What is more, I took it.

Nowadays I don't have those problems. I don't make an appearance on the greensward until June is nearly out and only then if the sun is melting the big roller. When on the field, I turn my arm over from a standing position and field at first slip, standing so close to the wicket-keeper that often I am to be found behind him. As a batsman I am delighted if I can hit far enough to call 'wait' to my partner. I am, to quote J.J. Warr (and one must never tire of quoting the classics), in the spring-time of my sporting senility.

What you never lose is the keen anticipation of the new season. One Saturday I walked round our ground and by the time I had travelled from one sightscreen to the other it had gone from bright but chilly sunshine to sleet being driven on a wind with the cutting edge of a chainsaw. The outfield has sand on it where the hockey players have been, the seats need a lick of paint, the hedges are bare of leaf. Swept by sleet and rain, the ground had a desolate look.

Any outsider witnessing the scene would think it an unseemly introduction to a game of such elegant repu-tation. What those of us who know realise is that there

will soon be days of unending summer when we shall see white warriors on green meadows. There will also be days when the drone of summer, the smell of cut grass, and the sound of cricket will produce a cocktail so potent that a sip could be fatal. What happens is you pass out in a deckchair. And when you wake up you think you've died and gone to heaven.

The marvellous thing about cricket is that you can have a better time when it rains than when it shines. In other words, often the conversation is an improvement on the cricket.

Visiting the Long Room bar one day I came across Alan Revill, of Derbyshire and Leicestershire, and Keith Andrew, of Northants and England. Mr Revill is one of those people who lives his life according to the cricket season. It is not known what he does during the football season, although it has been rumoured that he hibernates. When asked how long he has been married he will say he 'opened the innings in 1953'.

In a restaurant he will ask the waitress for 'the batting order' (the menu) and the 'score card' (the bill). We once spent a glorious summer day together, drinking good wine and telling tales. When the time came to go he surveyed my garden, cocked an ear to the birds, raised his face to the sun and said, 'I think we'll bat, Parky old lad.'

That day at Lord's we talked of life's mysteries, like how George Henry Pope bowled his leg-cutter and why Leslie Jackson, who took more than 1,700 first-class wickets at a cost of little over 17 apiece, played only

twice for England. This led us to ask the same of Mr Andrew who, although by common consent the finest wicket-keeper of his generation, also played only twice for his country.

Keith's first Test was against Australia at Brisbane in the 1954–55 series when England lost by an innings and 154 runs and went on to win the next three games in what became known as Tyson's series. Keith said that Tyson was at his quickest when something or someone upset him. When this happened, Keith said, it was advisable to move back five yards or so.

I once asked Keith Miller how quick Tyson was. Keith said he couldn't tell because he never managed to see a ball he bowled him.

I also asked Dennis Lillee what was the quickest he had ever bowled; he said the fastest ball he ever delivered was during a league game when he was playing in Lancashire. The unfortunate batsman was struck on the leg by Lillee's missile, a swinging yorker, whereupon the Australian appealed. The umpire gave the batsman out but, much to Lillee's annoyance, he didn't move. 'You're out,' Dennis said (or words to that effect).

The batsman looked at the bowler through pain-filled eyes and said, 'I'd love to go, Dennis, but I daren't move. I think you've broken my bloody leg.' And he had.

'Time to put the covers on,' said Mr Revill, by way of announcing that we would need an umbrella to get to the car park. We splashed by the Grace Gates. Glancing back through the rain, Lord's looked like a moated

castle. The next day they abandoned play. This was the sign we had all been waiting for; confirmation at last that the cricket season had begun.

April 1991

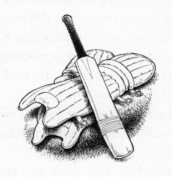

BARNSLEY CRICKET
GROUND

News item: *'Barnsley Cricket Club, who number Geoffrey Boycott, Dickie Bird and Martyn Moxon among their former players, may be forced to leave their ground midway through next season. The lease under which they have paid a peppercorn rent for over 50 years expires on August 1 and the owners of the ground, a local charitable trust, have offered a new three-year lease at £22,750 a year. A spokesman for the Trust said: 'We have sympathy with the club but we have been advised by the Charity Commission that we have to obtain the best possible income for the charity for the nine acres of land near the centre of Barnsley.'*

SOUNDS ominous. Nine acres near the middle of Barnsley. Make a lovely car park, or a hypermarket, or a car park for a hypermarket. Whatever happens, you can bet any money that it won't be what it has been these past fifty years or more: a proper cricket ground.

It wasn't some odd patch of grass on which cricket was played or an acre or two of grazing pasture with a wicket on it. It was, and is, a real cricket ground with a scoreboard, a substantial pavilion and the truest wicket I ever batted on. It is no coincidence that the three best known cricketers it produced – Boycott, Moxon and

Bird – were all opening bats. They learned on the perfect surface.

I joined the club forty years ago. In those days you auditioned and waited for the call. The decision was sometimes one of life or death because the wickets we played on in the local leagues around Barnsley were death traps. We would have had a better chance of survival playing on the main line between Doncaster and Kings Cross.

My local club, where I grew up watching my father and later playing with him, was located in a farmer's backyard with cornfields on the boundary and daisies and buttercups in the outfield. The pavilion was made of wood and we had a huge teapot, enamelled and bottomless.

Then we moved two fields away on to a brand new sports complex and for a while the pitch was a nightmare. Before the opening we instructed our groundsman, Old Cheyney, to produce a surface good enough to last for the official ceremony.

After that we would have to take our chances. His remedy was a strip concocted of marl and horse manure. 'Oss muck. There's nowt like it,' he'd say. He rolled it flat and let it set and although it looked an odd colour it certainly made a presentable batting surface.

On the day of the opening it rained and Cheyney's masterpiece became an evil-smelling quagmire which necessitated the police evacuating people from their nearby homes. What is more, in receiving the ceremonial first ball to declare our new ground officially open, our

captain played forward to a delivery of no great menace and lost his teeth.

This was not quite as dramatic as it sounds because the ball didn't hit him in the mouth but just below the heart. In fact, exactly on the breast pocket of his shirt which is where he stored his teeth while batting.

Some time later we entertained the Barnsley Second XI. This was important. This was us against the Folks Who Lived On The Hill. More importantly, this was my audition piece.

Our opening bowler at the time was a big lad called Terry MacDonald who was a pro boxer, and a good one. He was also quick and on our wicket unplayable and lethal. The Barnsley batsmen, coached to move into line with the head behind the ball, soon realised that such a technique would guarantee them a bed in the local infirmary.

They were chopped down but they didn't argue. For one thing Terry was too big but they also knew we had to play them on their patch. 'Let us see how good you are on a proper wicket,' is what they said.

I can remember to this day what it was like arriving at the ground. There was a man on the gate taking money. The scoreboard was like you saw at county grounds with an operator and individual as well as team scores so you needn't keep count in your head. I always did just in case the scorers missed a run. So did Geoffrey Boycott. But he auditioned later.

The dressing-room had enough pegs for all of us and hot and cold running water. And when you walked

down the steps in front of the pavilion you passed
through a little gate on the way to the wicket. And what
a wicket. Subsequently I played on all of Yorkshire's
county grounds and later on most of our Test grounds
and can honestly say that the wicket at Shaw Lane was
as good as any. If you could play straight, you could
hang around for a long time with a walking stick. I did
a lot of hanging around in the next few seasons. I wasn't
much of a stroke player but I could certainly loiter.

This characteristic was noted during my audition performance by a man sitting by the sightscreen. Having
observed me for about half an hour he shouted, 'I don't
know thi' name, lad, but I have to tell thi' tha's got
about as much life as a bloody tombstone.' I got to
know him well over the coming season. He always sat
in the same place and never changed his opinion of me.

As I walked to the wicket he would say in a loud
voice, 'Oh God, not 'im again.' He was merciless but
not particular. Anyone and everyone who played for
Barnsley at that time suffered. He had a running feud
with our skipper and pro, a nuggety little man called
Ernie Steele. At that time the Barnsley Club, with com-
mendable courage, had decided to blood young players
in the first team. It was a brave decision because the
Yorkshire League is one of the strongest and most competitive leagues in the land. It was also at a time when
people used to watch league cricket, so we had our
supporters to think of.

What it really meant was that Ernie Steele had a
thankless task which he performed with great skill and

forebearance. But there were times when the situation got the better of him. I remember playing once at Castleford, I think it was, against a young and fearsome quick bowler called Broughton who later played county cricket for Leicestershire.

I opened and didn't get too many in my half of the wicket from Mr Broughton, the majority of his deliveries bouncing way above my head. It wasn't that dangerous, but, on the other hand, it made scoring difficult. At the fall of a wicket Ernie Steele made his way to the middle carrying a pair of step ladders. It was a fair point to make but it wasn't very subtle. And it did much to improve Mr Broughton's aim.

During this period when we didn't win many games, Ernie took some terrible stick from our regular barracker. I remember one match when we were getting a pasting in the field and every time the opposition hit a boundary our barracker would shout, 'Put a man theer Ernie.'

After this had been going on for some time Ernie lost his temper and rounding on his critic bellowed from the centre of the field, 'And how many bloody fielders does tha' reckon I've got?' There was a pause and his critic shouted back, 'Not bloody sufficient.'

This wasn't the idyllic image of English club cricket. This wasn't about the smell of the cut grass and the gentle sound of leather on willow. This was altogether more rugged. This was the whiff of cordite and the sound of men at war. The rules were simple. Show no mercy, expect none in return; take no prisoners.

I don't even have to close my eyes to see players such as the magnificent young Boycott; the unrazored Dickie Bird, nervous as a grasshopper; the awesome Hubert Padgett, the best striker of a ball I ever saw at club level; or Graham Pearce, splayfooted, tireless, forever moaning but a marvellous bowler with the new ball. I remember fielding in the leg trap as Ellis Robinson bowled his off-spin and watching in awe as George Barnett at cover point swooped and threw his flat, whistling throw to the top of the stumps.

I remember the wind coming over the hill and the noise from Oakwell when the season overlapped. I remember learning the most beautiful of games in the best possible manner: on a decent wicket playing with men who knew.

If the time comes when there is no longer a cricket pitch at Shaw Lane it will be a tragedy for the community and for Yorkshire cricket.

The Charity Commission says that the Shawlands Trust, which owns the ground, should get the best possible income for the charity. Is it not also the purpose of a local charity to be concerned about how best it can serve the people of the local community?

Anyone who has even the beginning of an idea about changing the use of the ground from anything other than a place where cricket is played should be aware that they are contemplating sacrilege. They should also know that the place is guarded by ghosts and that they are in danger of suffering the Curse of Parkinson.

They should tread softly. They are on hallowed ground.

1994

In 1996 Barnsley Rugby Club bought the ground from Shaw-lands Trust; one of the stipulations was that Barnsley Cricket Club could continue to use the ground, and this saved them from extinction.

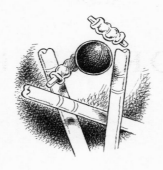

YORKSHIRE

HEADINGLEY

I HAVE never been stuck on Headingley. The best cricket grounds have imposing pavilions: Lord's, Old Trafford, Trent Bridge. At Leeds, the players emerge from a hole in the back of the rugby stand – hardly the entry of gladiators. Additions to the ground have only served to make it seem more higgledy-piggledy in appearance.

There is nothing gracious about it. Headingley is irredeemably plain. Yorkshire cricket deserves a more imposing home than the rented accommodation it presently occupies. That the Yorkshire club doesn't own an acre of the county it represents tells an awful lot about the manner in which the club was run in the past.

Nonetheless, for all its faults, it is an evocative place to visit. I first went to Headingley in 1948 and saw Bradman's Australians, then more than halfway through their victorious rampage of the country. The first day of that famous match I sat in the sun on the seats where the old winter shed used to be. Ray Illingworth watched all five days from the same place. In those days, we didn't know each other but shared the same dreams, worshipped the same heroes.

Our big hero, Len Hutton, opened the innings with Washbrook against Miller and Lindwall and they put on 168, Len making 81 and Washbrook 143. The selectors brought Hutton back for Headingley having dropped

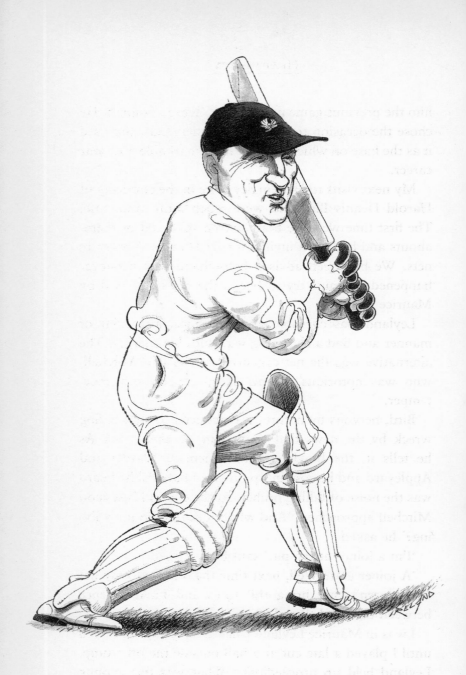

Len Hutton

him the previous game in favour of George Emmett. He chose the occasion to demonstrate their folly and used it as the base on which he built his remarkable post-war career.

My next visits to Headingley were in the company of Harold Dennis Bird and were much more traumatic. The first time we were both sixteen years old or thereabouts and had been invited for trials to the Yorkshire nets. We had been advised beforehand that whatever happened we must try to bat in the net supervised by Maurice Leyland.

Leyland was cherubic of appearance, avuncular of manner and had a charming way with his charges. The alternative was the net organised by 'Ticker' Mitchell, who was notorious for his sharp tongue and short temper.

Bird, nervous by nature, was reduced to a gibbering wreck by the news that he was in Mitchell's net. As he tells it, the bowlers were Trueman, Wardle and Appleyard and he couldn't put bat on ball. All he heard was the noise of falling timber. At the end of his session Mitchell approached. 'And what does tha' do for a living?' he asked.

'I'm a joiner at the pit,' said Bird.

'A joiner is it? Well, next time tha' comes to my net why doesn't tha' bring thi' tools and build a fence between thee and t'bowler?' said Mitchell.

I was in Maurice Leyland's net. Everything went well until I played a late cut at a ball outside the off stump. Leyland held up proceedings. 'What was that, young

man?' he asked. 'A late cut, Mr Leyland,' I told him. He shook his head sadly at the folly of it all. I felt like I had been caught smoking behind the bike sheds.

Bird felt worse than I did when we returned to Barnsley. In fact, he was invited back and went on to become a professional cricketer. On the other hand, I never heard from the Yorkshire County Cricket Club again. So much for that nice Mr Leyland and that horrible 'Ticker' Mitchell.

The next time I accompanied Bird to Headingley we were opening the innings for Barnsley against Leeds. The Yorkshire League in those days was a tough league to play in.

Every team had their quota of battle-hardened pros and young aspirants for a Yorkshire cap. Our anticipation of walking out to bat at Headingley was diminished somewhat by the news that Trueman was in the Leeds side.

In those days, Trueman was in the process of making his fearsome reputation as a bowler of genuine pace. As I remember events, he burst through Bird's defences with a ball of exceptional pace that took him just below the heart and felled him.

After I had tended my stricken colleague, got him to his feet and put the bat back in his hand, I walked back to my crease, passing on the way Trueman, who had been observing Bird's recuperation.

'Is he all right?' asked Trueman, pleasantly. 'I think so,' I said. He nodded, gripped the ball with the seam

showing and said, 'Good. Now think on lad, you're next.'

August 1994

Yorkshire had hoped to move to a new, purpose-built ground at the junction of the MI and M62 in the late nineties but the funding proved insufficient. New stands have since been erected at Headingley. The expenditure required to ensure that Leeds remains a Test-match venue is a heavy burden for Yorkshire CCC.

ROSES MATCHES

I was twelve before they let me watch a Roses game. I had been to the cricket before – I had already seen such wonders as Constantine fielding, Compton batting and Miller bowling – but these were fripperies compared to the real thing.

Being allowed to go to a game between Yorkshire and Lancashire was an important ritual in growing up; like having your first pint or using a razor or wearing long pants.

My father took me to Bramall Lane in 1947 where we sat on the football terraces for the best part of the day through sunshine and rain, not daring to move but also not wanting to. There were 22,000 people in Bramall Lane that Saturday so long ago in conditions that nowadays would necessitate a public inquiry.

When my father stood up to go to the toilet he walked like Groucho Marx. Yet none of us would have swapped our concrete perch for a seat in Paradise that Saturday in August 1947.

Yorkshire batted first. Hutton opened with Keighley who soon departed. Pollard and Phillipson were bowling well. The great Len was defending grimly and we settled down for a few hours of trench warfare. The crowd were happy.

This was Yorkshire v. Lancashire and things were as they should be. Into the arena strode young Gerald

Smithson. It was his first Roses game. He had already been given his instructions by Emmott Robinson who had told him to 'stick thi' bat in t'block-hole and leave it there at all costs'.

This was sound advice from one who knew. Instead, Mr Smithson played as if on the beach at Bridlington. He carted Phillipson for three fours and a three in one over. He was like a greyhound in a Donkey Derby. He missed his century by two runs but there will be those at Bramall Lane that day who still remember Smithson's 98 long after they have forgotten a dozen or more less dramatic centuries.

According to reports, the only person who was less than impressed by Smithson's innings was the aforesaid Emmott Robinson. As Smithson put Lancashire to the sword, Emmott was heard to mutter, 'He'll nivver learn, yon lad; he'll nivver learn.'

The contest was a draw, which is what was expected of Roses games in those days. It was not so much a cricket match as a ceremony between two great tribes.

Since my initiation, I have travelled far and wide, seen cricket in many countries and witnessed remarkable events, but none remain as vivid in my memory as the Yorkshire v. Lancashire games of my youth.

Little did I know as I watched events unfurl at Bramall Lane there were one or two people on the field I would come to know in later life. If someone had told me that one day I would sit next to Len Hutton at dinner and talk about the art of batting I would have said they were mad. And yet I did.

Many years later I asked him what he thought of modern players. 'Don't use their feet enough. They should watch Fred Astaire,' he said.

I remembered this when I interviewed Mr Astaire. I wanted to tell him about Len Hutton but I thought it might confuse him, particularly as I would have to confess that when I saw him dance with Rita Hayworth in *You Were Never Lovelier* I could only compare it to Len Hutton's cover drive. Nor could I have known that Ellis Robinson, the Yorkshire off-spinner who all but did for Lancashire that day at Bramall Lane, was to be my team-mate at Barnsley three or four years later when he retired from county cricket.

I remember fielding for him in the leg trap when he was bowling at a slogger who cared little for reputation and whose only ambition was to kill forward short-leg.

As I retreated under the onslaught, Mr Robinson kept urging me closer. Finally, I was struck a terrible blow on the kneecap and, as I lay on the ground in need of medical attention and sympathy, I was approached by the man responsible for my predicament.

I expected Mr Robinson to show some concern. Instead he stood over me and said, 'Tha' stands abart as if thi' knickers were starched.' I took this to mean that my wounds were self-inflicted.

It was three years after Bramall Lane that I first visited Old Trafford. You must remember that in 1950 a journey from Barnsley to Manchester was like an adventure to another planet. It required all the planning of a space probe.

Our means of transport was an ancient Triumph motor car, lately acquired by my father, which had never been over the Pennines. It was a strange-looking contraption, mainly because it sloped. This was because my father had replaced the springs at the rear of the car with some he had found in a scrapyard. I think they came from a double-decker bus because they lifted the back so that the car appeared to be pointed downwards. Sitting in the back seat was a bit like being in a roller-coaster on a steep descent.

I don't know what time we set off in the morning, but I do know it was dark. We arrived at Old Trafford at 7 a.m. so by the time play started at 11.30 I had been up so long I was ready for bed. Lancashire had a new bowler playing in his first Roses game. Brian Statham was his name. 'What's he like?' we asked our neighbours. They didn't know. But we soon found out.

He bowled Frank Lowson for a duck and did for Ted Lester in a similar fashion. Roy Tattersall dismissed Len Hutton and, before we knew it, Yorkshire were 40 odd for five and the young Statham had taken three for very few. It was our first view of that supple, whirling action which became the trademark of his quality. Did he ever bowl a long hop? I doubt it.

Norman Yardley rescued us that day with a century and once more the game was drawn. Statham apart, the significance of that trip was that it introduced me to Old Trafford and to Manchester, my favourite ground in my favourite northern city.

I also clapped eyes on Malcolm Hilton for the first time. Malcolm was a slow left-arm bowler who had achieved celebrity status by twice dismissing Don Bradman in 1948. This was an achievement comparable with having discovered penicillin and composing *As Time Goes By* on the same day.

When I learned that Malcolm had died I was greatly saddened because he was one of those rare men who cause you to smile at their memory. He was a Lancashire hotpot of a man: his accent was plump and juicy; he had a tasty wit. He sometimes opened the bowling for Lancashire. Indeed, he did that day at Old Trafford against Yorkshire.

Those were the days when teams had spin bowlers instead of phantom seamers. He was a marvellous fielder, particularly close to the wicket when Tattersall was bowling. Hilton, Ikin and Grieves didn't miss much in the leg trap.

But Malcolm's great gift was as a teller of tales. He was droll with a faultless style. I once asked him about Tattersall and he said, 'Tha' could reckon he'd bowl one bad ball a year. I were t'spotter for t'leg trap. I fielded at backward short-leg so I could see where Tatt was going to pitch it. If it were short I'd shout "duck lads!" and they'd know to get out of the way.

'One Pancake Tuesday Tatt bowled a long hop. I spotted it but I thought I'd have a bit of fun so I didn't call it. Well t'batsman got hold of it and gave t'ball a terrible thump. Tha' should have seen Jack Ikin's face. He didn't speak to me for three months.'

'Did it hit him?' I asked. 'No, he caught it,' said Malcolm.

If ever a Lowry landscape needed a description then Malcolm Hilton's would have been the perfect voice. He ruminated on life with lugubrious wit. Anything would get him going.

I was sulking after missing a catch and he said, 'One season I were in t'leg trap and were copping everything and Washy [Cyril Washbrook] says to me, "Does tha' reckon thissen at cover, Malcolm?" And I said, cocky as anything, "Tha' knows me, Skipper. I can catch 'em anywhere."

'So I trot off to cover and this batsman gets reight under one from Tatt and up and up she goes until she's higher than Blackpool Tower and I'm running to get under her.

'Well I'd been runnin' like a stag for two minutes and she's still going up but now she's started drifting, going this way and that and I'm under her running round in circles thinkin' "booger this".

'And then t'bloody thing starts dropping and I'm still running all over t'place but now I'm shouting, "It's mine, it's mine, it's mine," to get t'others out of the way.

'By this time I've got no idea where I am. All I know as t'ball gets nearer is I'm not properly under it so as it falls I dive forward. Next thing I know I've knocked down t'wicket-keeper, one set of stumps, two men in t'leg trap and t'umpire at square-leg. And I've still missed t'ball by ten feet.

'So I'm lying theer among all t'debris – it were like a battlefield – and I look up and theer's t'skipper looking down at me. And he says, "By the way Hilton, does tha' know any other daft tricks?"'

The character of men like Malcolm Hilton and Ellis Robinson was at the soul of the Roses games.

I haven't been to one lately because it has all changed – not just the cricket, but the rest of it. I listened to the radio commentary of last week's one-day semi-final and was glad I wasn't there, not because Yorkshire lost but because, according to the commentators, there was ill feeling on the field.

One or two of the Lancashire players were petulant when Metcalfe was given not out and none of them applauded his century. This is not as it should be, and certainly not as it was.

What gave the Roses games their particular competitive edge was that each side had respect for the other. That might have disappeared and, if it has, the worse it is for players and spectators alike.

Tawdry behaviour is best forgotten. Not even a poet like Malcolm Hilton could incorporate it into the legend of Yorkshire versus Lancashire.

If the modern player wants a guide to what it used to be like, then let me tell him about Ken Taylor making his debut in a Roses game at Old Trafford in the 1960s. He went out to face a rampant Statham who had just dismissed two Yorkshire batsmen for no runs.

In those days there used to be a gate attendant at Old Trafford. As Ken walked out with the Lancashire crowd

baying for blood, the gateman said, 'Good luck, young man. But think on, don't be long.'

Ken was still pondering this instruction as Statham ran in and bowled him first ball. Ken walked back to the pavilion, whereupon the same attendant opened the gate, doffed his cap and said, 'Thank you, lad.'

YORKSHIRE'S NEW REGIME

DAVID BYAS is as sturdy and rugged a York-shireman as you will find and he will need all his strength and patience when he takes over as the new captain of his county. It used to be the ultimate honour guaranteeing a place in the pantheon. For the past twenty years or so it has been a nightmare occupation making the incumbent wish he had chosen a safe job like training pit bulls or being Mike Tyson's sparring partner.

The task before David Byas is simple. He has about five years in which to win the County Championship, something the team haven't done since 1968. Twenty-seven years without a sniff would be bad for a team of modest reputation and ability but for one of the most famous and successful teams in the history of cricket it represents a calamity.

Why has it happened? In my view the real reason is that the very qualities beloved by Yorkshiremen – the strong sense of tradition, the bloody-mindedness, the tribal pride – have all prevented necessary change and stunted development.

In the fifties and sixties there was no reason to doubt that Yorkshire had the formula for success. Winning was a time-honoured tradition based on continuity and pride. It meant that if they needed a new fast bowler, they whistled down the pit-shaft and up came Fred Trueman.

If they wanted a successor to Len Hutton, they looked no further than Barnsley and found Geoff Boycott.

Tough leaders? Well Brian Sellars begat Brian Close. Don Wilson took over from Johnny Wardle, John Hampshire for Vic Wilson. There were Illingworth, Stott, Taylor, Sharpe, Binks, Old and Nicholson and many others with an ability and know-how unmatched by any other county. The supply seemed never-ending. It was deemed God-given.

Yorkshire felt no need to contemplate change. While every other county strengthened its team by recruiting overseas players, Yorkshire stuck to its tradition of only playing people born in the broad acres. It was a sentiment as dangerous as it was phoney.

It was dangerous because it underestimated the effect importing the world's best players would have on the County Championship, and bogus because long before the club decided on an open policy in the 1990s, well over twenty cricketers not born in Yorkshire had worn the White Rose.

That the majority of these imposters were gentlemen rather than players (in the old-fashioned cricketing sense) did considerable damage to another Yorkshire boast, that Yorkshire cricket was entirely classless.

Someone once claimed there would be a man on the moon before Yorkshire employed a foreign player – and that much at least was true. In fact, it was some time after the giant step for mankind had been taken that the Yorkshire Committee took what it regarded as an equally dramatic step into the future.

By the time Sachin Tendulkar became Yorkshire's first official outsider in 1992, a generation had grown up in the county which knew only of Yorkshire's glories by listening to the memories of old men. Even worse, there were players who spent an entire career with a county without winning a sausage.

In these barren years the county lost direction as well as the winning habit. The great players of the past seemed to prefer arguing with one another rather than making a positive contribution to the future of the club. One of the great unanswered mysteries of our time is how a county that could call on a Brains Trust as knowledgeable and talented as Close, Illingworth, Boycott and Trueman could seem so hapless and short of ideas. I remember interviewing Martyn Moxon in 1994 and him shaking his head and saying, 'Think what it might have been like if Fred coached Darren Gough or Geoff sorted out one or two of our younger batsmen.'

After six years, Moxon – as good and as decent a cricketer as you will come across – had had enough. He resigned the captaincy, seeing he had given up telling the team what to do because they had stopped listening to him. At least in Moxon's reign the bickering had stopped – or quietened at least – and a new president, Sir Laurence Byford, had started exerting an imposing authority.

However, the main problem remains. How do Yorkshire return to winning ways? Byas will give a fresh voice and determination but the significant decision was to advertise for a coach/manager. Where the search leads might tell us if Yorkshire have finally managed to escape

the siege mentality that has hampered the team for so long.

Chris Hassell, the chief executive, says the search for the right man will extend overseas. I hope so.

If there is to be a change then let it be radical. Let the county find someone who arrives in Yorkshire unencumbered by the history and traditions of the club, someone who knows nothing about and cares even less for the factions within the county and their silly feuds.

Boycott tells the story of suggesting, some time ago, that Malcolm Marshall coach the Yorkshire bowlers. 'But he's black isn't he?' said a committee man. 'He was last time I looked,' said Geoff.

The committee man wasn't being racist, merely insular, and it is that lack of vision, that narrow-minded belief that if it's not home-grown it won't do, that has caused Yorkshire cricket lovers so much despair for near-on thirty years.

Time for a change. Time to be bold. After all, they have nothing to lose. Not since 1968 they haven't.

October 1995

David Byas led Yorkshire to the Championship in 2001, the county's first win in the competition for thirty-three years. Wayne Clark from Western Australia, the county's first overseas coach, oversaw the victory. At the end of the season, Byas retired (although he later accepted an invitation to captain Lancashire in 2002) and Yorkshire appointed their overseas player Darren Lehmann from South Australia as his successor.

YORKSHIREMEN

Wilfred Rhodes – the Peerless Professional

Wilfred Rhodes is in his nineties and still a young man. It was my grandfather who first told me about him. He once walked the thirty miles to Bradford to see Rhodes play and he never forgot it.

Rhodes didn't let him down. 'He took six or seven wickets that day without breakin' sweat and I said to a bloke sitting next to me, "How's tha' reckon he'll do in t'second innings?" and he says, "T'same," and I said, "How's tha' know?" and he said, "If Wilfred does thi' once, he'll do thi' aggean. He's spotted thi' weakness tha' sees, and if he's done that, tha's bound to be Wilfred's next time round." And he was right tha' knows. Next innings he did t'same. Ah, he was a good 'un, Wilfred. Tha' could walk thirty miles and reckon on him doing summat.'

Throughout his career Wilfred Rhodes specialised in always 'doing summat'. When he retired from the game he had scored 39,802 runs and taken 4,187 wickets. Only ten batsmen in the history of the game have scored more runs and no bowler has come within a thousand wickets of Rhodes. Only George Hirst is within two of his sixteen doubles of 1,000 runs and 100 wickets in the same season, only Tich Freeman within six of his twenty-three years of taking 100 wickets and no one else has ever twice made over 2,000 runs in a season and three times taken over 200 wickets.

Wilfred Rhodes

As Sir Neville Cardus wrote: 'The man's life and deeds take the breath away.' His career began with him playing against W.G. Grace in Victoria's reign and ended in the thirties when he played against Bradman. He played first-class cricket for thirty-two years, surviving every changing fashion in the game, shrugging off every potential challenger to his crown. Even today, at the age of ninety, the crown is still his.

I never saw Wilfred Rhodes play cricket. He had been retired seventeen years when I saw my first Yorkshire game but I fancy I knew more about his deeds than I did about the other players who took the field that summer's day in 1947. My grandfather and my father had crammed my young head with tales about him. I first saw him at the Scarborough Festival. Indeed, I measured off my youth with visits to Scarborough to see the Festival and gaze in awe at Wilfred Rhodes.

And later, much later, when my job gave me the excuse, I dared to sit with him. By then he was blind, listening to the cricket and talking to Bob Appleyard. Jackie Hampshire was batting and he struck a ball massively over the square-leg boundary, his bat making a sound like a hammer hitting an anvil. Wilfred stopped his discourse. 'I'll bet that went some way,' he said. Appleyard said, 'Six over square-leg. Jackie was sweeping.' Wilfred said scornfully, 'Sweeping. That nivver was any sort of shot. Once I was listening to television and a cricketer was coaching youngsters how to sweep. I had to switch it off.'

I remembered that Rhodes, after retiring from the

county game, had coached at Harrow and asked him if he enjoyed it. 'It was all right,' he said, 'but them young lads were overcoached when they came to me. Tha' could always tell what they'd do, allus forward, ever forward. I used to run up to bowl and not let go and theer they'd be on t'front foot, leg stretched down t'wicket. And I'd walk up to 'em and say, "Na' then, lad, wheers tha' going? Off for a walk perhaps?"'

He shook his head sorrowfully. 'Tha' knows one thing I learned about cricket: tha' can't put in what God left out. Tha' sees two kind of cricketers, them that uses a bat as if they are shovelling muck and them that plays proper, and like as not God showed both of them how to play.'

I remarked how strange it seemed that he, the quintessential Yorkshire professional, the man who 'laiked proper' and 'not for fun', should teach cricket at one of the temples of the amateur game.

'Lads were all right,' he said. 'I liked them, we got on well. It was t'others, t'masters, I couldn't get on with. They allus thought they knew more than me. I told one of 'em one day he'd been interferin' and I said, "Tha' can't know more about this game than me tha' knows," and he said, "Why not?" and I said, "Because if thi' did tha'd be playing for England and I'd be doing thi' job teaching Greek."'

Listening to Rhodes one is transported to a world where cricketers wore sidewhiskers and starched the cuffs of their shirts; a game of gentlemen and players, separate entrances, attitudes as different as night and

day. Because his mind sees them clearly, he introduces you to Trumper and Ranji and Grace and Gregory and Armstrong and Plum Warner. He can conjure up cricket in Victorian England, in the First World War, through the depression years to the 'Golden Thirties'. He is a walking history of the game, blessed with a fabulous memory and the unequivocal attitude of one who is certain of what he says for the simple reason that he was there when it happened. When Wilfred Rhodes tells you that Bradman was the best bat who ever lived and that S.F. Barnes was the best bowler, only the foolish would dare argue.

'It's a thinking game is cricket. If tha' doesn't use thi' brains tha' might as well give up. When I took up batting serious and opened wi' Jack Hobbs in Australia, a lot said I couldn't bat. But I thought about it and decided that t'best way to go about t'job in Australia was to play forward. In that trip I made one or two [including a record opening partnership of 323 with Hobbs] and one day I'm going on t'tram to t'ground and Duff, t'Australian cricketer, sits next to me and starts chatting. He said, "Tha' knows tha' baffles me, Wilfred," and I said, "How come?" and he says, "Well, tha's got all these runs on this tour and yet tha' can't bat. Tha's only got one shot." And I said, "Ay, and that's all I need out here." Same with bowling, too, although you could say I was more gifted than most at it. But I still used to think 'em out. Batsmen used to say about me that I could drop a ball on a sixpence. Now that's impossible, no one can do that. I could probably hit a newspaper,

spread out at that. But point is they used to think I could hit a sixpence and I used to let 'em keep on thinking and that way they were mine.'

During our talk he riffled through the years, illuminating forgotten summers with his yarns, breathing life into cricketers long dead. About M.A. Noble, the great Australian all-rounder who captained his country at the turn of the century, he said, 'That Noble was a good 'un. Used to bowl his quicker one with his fingers straight up t'seam. He nivver got me.' On Geoffrey Boycott, who played for England seventy years later, 'I said to him one day, "Does tha' cut?" And he said, "A bit," and I said, "Remember not to do it until May's finished."'

He lives with his daughter Muriel and her husband Tom near Bournemouth. He still enjoys good health, takes a daily walk and listens to the radio. During the cricket season he keeps in touch with the game with occasional trips to Lord's where he meets old friends eager for a yarn. His encyclopaedic mind is fed daily by fresh facts on cricket read to him from the papers by his daughter and son-in-law.

He doesn't miss a trick. I once wrote a story for the *Sunday Times* about an incident concerning W.G. Grace. During a Gentlemen versus Players fixture at Lord's, Schofield Haigh, the Yorkshire player, asked the good doctor's permission to leave the field early on the last afternoon so that he might journey back to Yorkshire. Permission was granted. On that last afternoon as the time for Haigh's departure and Grace's century drew nigh, Grace hit an easy catch toward Haigh. As

Haigh awaited the ball, the doctor shouted, 'Take the catch and you miss the train.' Not being daft Haigh missed the catch and in consequence was home in Yorkshire when he wanted to be.

Shortly after writing the story I received a letter. It simply said, 'That story you told about Schofield Haigh was true. I know because I was the bowler.' It was signed Wilfred Rhodes. I still have it. I wouldn't swap it for a gold pig.

It's not everyone who gets a letter from the gods.

Wilfred Rhodes died at his Hampshire home in July 1973 aged ninety-five. Until the advent of Garfield Sobers, Rhodes was probably the greatest all-rounder in the game's history.

Brian Close – captain courageous

BRIAN CLOSE to Imran Khan, who glides forward and strikes the ball back over the bowler's head for six. He does it twice more in the over as well as sweeping for four. The last straight drive is the best. Imran poses in the follow-through, the bat high, the profile of a hawk.

John Arlott might have been moved to verse. Brian Close took a more pragmatic view of things. 'I never could bowl to a bloody slogger,' he said, taking his sweater.

Dennis Brian Close was well into his seventh decade at the time, but still battling, still playing a charity game as if his life depended upon it. He is seventy next week but you don't have to believe it. I don't. Neither does the birthday boy.

He remains the cocksure, cockeyed wunderkind who was capped for England before he wore the White Rose and who, in a different and more enlightened time, would have represented his country fifty or sixty more times than he did.

In fact, he played twenty-two Tests for England and led them on seven occasions without defeat. That's respectable but it doesn't reflect his talent as an all-rounder and captain. In his long career, Close scored nigh on 35,000 runs, took almost 1,200 wickets and held more than 800 catches.

In his youth he excited spectators in a manner only

seen since in the emerging Botham. He bowled fast, smote sixes, fielded fearlessly. This was, and is, a majestic athlete. He played football as a professional and could have played golf for a living, achieving single-figure handicaps both left- and right-handed. He was a formidable opponent at tennis and squash. Any game comes naturally to him.

As a natural leader of men, a warrior setting the example for the rest to follow, there have been few to match him. Illingworth was shrewder, more patient and cunning; Close was the gambler, imaginative, impulsive, often reckless.

Close, Illingworth and Fred Trueman were the inspiration of the Yorkshire team of the sixties. With Close in charge, Yorkshire won four County Championships and only the Surrey side led by Stuart Surridge could challenge their claim to be the best county side in that silver period linking the post- and pre-war games.

The former England coach and Lancashire player David Lloyd has stated that just the sight of a Yorkshire team filing in for lunch in their blazers in those days was enough to convince the opposition they didn't have a chance.

The players under Brian Close were as argumentative, bloody-minded and disputatious as you would normally expect to find in a Yorkshire dressing-room but no one doubted who was the boss. Close's knowledge of the opposition was comprehensive and acute. He had a theory for every situation. He was bold and innovative.

On the other hand he could drift away into a private

world where he began practising golf shots, much to the amusement of his team-mates who regarded him as an eccentric uncle, an inspiration one moment and daft as a brush the next.

Most of all he was fearless. No one stood closer to the batsman than Brian Close. No other player can claim to have been battered as much as he.

Nowadays close fielders wear shin pads and helmets and rightly so. Brian Close would regard them as cissies. He never flinched nor admitted discomfort.

When struck on the shin once from a thumping on-drive, he moved closer. At the end of the over his boot was full of blood. 'Get on with it,' he told concerned team-mates.

On another occasion the ball, from a full-blooded pull shot, struck his forehead and was fielded first bounce by extra-cover. When the players picked their skipper up all he wanted to know was whether the fielder had caught the rebound.

Wes Hall and Charlie Griffiths once worked him over in a Test match at Lord's in 1963. Close scored 70 but took a terrible battering on his ribs. He returned the following day to play for Yorkshire where they took a colour photo of his bruising it was so spectacular. It looked like he had been hit by a truck. He went on to the field, bowled 25 overs and took 6 for 55. He scored 61 and then took another 4 wickets to lead his team to victory. All he said was, 'There is no such thing as pain.'

Close proved his theory again when at the age of

forty-five he was brought back by England and showed his courage against Holding, Andy Roberts and Wayne Daniel on a sub-standard pitch. Appropriately, he entitled his autobiography *I Don't Bruise Easily*.

There was much more to him than guts and will power. He was a subtle psychologist on the field of play. He didn't go in for the ugly, abusive sledging we see and hear nowadays. He chose a more artful approach. He would muse on the state of the game and the ability of his opponent to cope with what he had in store in the manner of a private conversation, just loud enough for the opposition to hear.

Not all Brian's theories worked, though. His idea that he could read the *Racing Post* while driving a car at 70 m.p.h. got him into terrible trouble. The only time team-mates dared refuse their captain was when he offered them a lift to a game.

He once swam the River Severn for a bet, and when visiting a Hollywood hotel wagered he could dive into the pool over a chair, which he easily accomplished. The bet escalated to the point where Close endeavoured to dive over three chairs and two tables, which ended with the hotel being short of poolside furniture for a while.

His dismissal by Yorkshire was cruel but somehow typical of the club at the time, dominated as it was by Brian Sellars whose management technique was as uncaring as it was unthinking.

On the other hand, it set Brian Close on a most improbable and glorious adventure at Somerset in the

company of two young rising stars called Botham and Richards. He showed the county how to win. Illingworth did the same at Leicestershire.

Their success and the subsequent decline of the county that sacked them only served to show the sub-standard nature of management at Yorkshire. Both men displayed their deep love for their native county by returning and trying to turn things round, but to no avail. County cricket had changed. So had the world.

Has Brian Close given up now he is a septuagenarian? Not likely. He still plays whenever he can and remains involved with the game and the club he loves. A young player spending time in his company would be left in no doubt that Mr Close is generally unimpressed by what he sees nowadays and that the game was better when he was a lad. Old warhorses are allowed their memories, even if they are rosy-hued.

On the other hand, it is unarguable that the Yorkshire side has never been the same since Close left, and the team he led could stand comparison with any in the history of Yorkshire cricket. That is how he should be remembered.

On his seventieth birthday Brian Close can be proud of the distinct and vigorous contribution he made to the game. He is entitled to feel short-changed by the dodos who picked England teams in his time but his reputation and his destiny belong in the clay that shaped him.

He was the last Yorkshireman to captain a team of fellow Yorkshiremen to beat all-comers.

You don't have to be born in Barnsley to recognise the importance of that achievement. But it helps.

February 2001

Brian Close remains associated with the development of young Yorkshire cricketers. His trenchant views are often sought out by the media when a new cricketing controversy arises, and his entertainment value remains as high on screen or in print as it was on the field of play.

GEOFFREY BOYCOTT – A
MAN AT ODDS

H E carries with him the air of a man perpetually at odds with the world. No one suffers the slings and arrows of outrageous fortune – real or imagined – more publicly than Geoff Boycott. When his recall to Test cricket was announced – surely a matter for personal joy – he was heard on television predicting that there would be many people hoping he would fail at Trent Bridge. This comment surprised no one who has closely observed The World versus Geoffrey Boycott over the past decade or so.

Of all the athletes I know, none has worked more assiduously to become the greatest player of his generation, and similarly no one of my acquaintance has paid so little attention to the inevitable consequences of succeeding in that ambition; namely, the business of being a public figure.

Geoffrey Boycott, who neither knows nor cares overmuch about anything else outside of cricket, would claim that his job was to play like the great cricketer he is and not bother about winning any charm contests. Yet there is little doubt – and he knows it, too – that his career in the game would have been a whole lot less turbulent and troublesome had he been able to apply to his life off the field the intelligence and tactical awareness he revealed on it.

Geoffrey Boycott's ruthless drive to succeed has cost him dearly in what might be termed his social development. At thirty-six and with fifteen or more years behind him of playing sport at the top-most level, meeting people from all areas of society, travelling the world, he can still be a gauche, uncertain figure – no more, you might say, than many other athletes with the same kind of experience, which is true, except that Geoffrey Boycott is much more intelligent than the average athlete. He has a keen, sharp mind, he is nobody's fool, and he takes nothing at face value, all of which Mr Kerry Packer will testify to be true. Boycott's refusal to take Packer's gold was not so much a patriotic gesture; more a careful decision taken after keen perusal of the small print in his contract. Those now locked in combat with Mr Packer and bemoaning the fact that they are unable to obtain a sight of one of these contracts should immediately contact Geoffrey Boycott. He has total recall of what his contained.

The paradox of Geoffrey Boycott is that the man who is absolutely self-sufficient in making such difficult decisions, who has mastered in his own way the intricacies of the most complex of games, is the same person who presents himself as a slightly bitter, embattled figure only at ease in the company of his own beloved Yorkshire team or the handful of people he trusts with complete friendship.

He is, at heart, a loner; more, I suspect, by the circumstances that shaped him rather than by any natural inclination. From the very first moment he played cricket in

the Yorkshire mining village where he was born he was determined not simply to play for Yorkshire and England but to be the pre-eminent batsman of his generation. In other words, his ambition was not simply a Yorkshire cap but the laurel wreaths worn by Sutcliffe and Hutton.

Typically, he pursued an alternative career to enter the civil service with the consequent result that throughout his early and late teens, when his contemporaries were indulging in all the possible joys of teenage life, Geoffrey Boycott's existence was divided equally between studying for examinations and practising cricket.

I met him first when he came to play for Barnsley at the age of fifteen. In those days, not fully fleshed out and wearing National Health spectacles, he looked an unlikely and puny recruit to a notoriously tough League which took no prisoners. But, from the beginning, he showed himself to be an exceptional talent with an insatiable appetite for learning the game. There was also in this period the first indication of the ruthless streak in his character that later led him into unhappy conflict with some fellow players and the executive.

The story goes that he was playing a friendly Sunday fixture and batting well when play was interrupted to hand him a message asking him to report the next day to Headingley to join the Yorkshire first-team squad. Geoffrey Boycott read the message and walked to the pavilion even though his innings was not finished. He was pursued to the pavilion gate by the opposing skipper

who, not unnaturally, pointed out that it was common courtesy to ask his permission before he left the field of play. Moreover, where was he going? Geoffrey Boycott looked at him and said, 'I've finished with this kind of cricket.' And he had.

The answer as to why he chose this course of action – and the answer to a lot of other questions about Geoffrey Boycott – was probably given much later in his career when, as England's opening batsman, he was *en route* to Australia with Mike Smith's team. Stopping over in Sri Lanka, every player in the party had to fill in a form stating, among other things, the purpose of their visit. Everyone completed the form by stating 'Cricket'; everyone, that is, except Geoffrey Boycott, who wrote 'Business'.

It is difficult for anyone, including fellow players, to comprehend Boycott's total absorption in the game he loves. His idea of relaxation is a three-hour net practice, his sole topic of conversation is cricket. He is single, teetotal, non-smoking and still living at home with his mother. In his obsessive dedication to physical fitness, his careful diet, his abhorrence of late nights, he further isolates himself from the majority of his fellow cricketers who as much enjoy the social side of the game as the playing of it.

He stands out like a Roundhead in a platoon of Cavaliers, and it is this dedication and pride in what he does and what he is that has taken him into the most troubled waters of his turbulent career. Certainly it was the reason for his self-imposed exile from Test cricket. Quite

simply, Geoffrey Boycott believed that one day he would be captain of England, not because it was his right, but because he was the best man for the job. He swallowed his pride under Denness because he calculated, and correctly, that the Kent player's days were numbered. It was when Greig was given the vice-captaincy that Boycott foresaw a future whereby he was kept from his ambition not only by a less experienced captain but, moreover, a foreign player. He was deeply hurt by what he considered to be an insulting rejection of his claims. Not for the first time in his life, he went his own lonely way.

What changed his mind was Greig's departure and pressure from people around him to display his great talents in the settings they deserve. Anyone who loves the game and delights in watching a great batsman at work can only rejoice at his return and hope that in his years away from Test cricket he has cultivated a more philosophical approach to his relationship with the game. In his darker moments he should remember the boy at Leeds who ran on to the pitch wearing a sweatshirt bearing the legend 'Boycott Bats On Water'. There are more cricket lovers in Britain who would go along with that sentiment than people who would like to see him sink.

If Geoffrey Boycott can loosen just a little the tight rein of his self-discipline and vaunting ambition, we might be lucky enough to see the re-emergence of a great international batsman in the Test arena, and, more importantly, the emergence of a remarkable man with a lot to offer cricket both on and off the field.

There are propitious signs. Recently Yorkshire were playing Nottinghamshire at Trent Bridge and bowling badly. In his endeavour to stem the flow of runs, Boycott was handicapped by injuries to two of his key bowlers. After retrieving the ball from the mid-wicket boundary, Boycott was addressed by a spectator who, in a loud voice, demanded to know why Robinson wasn't given a bowl. Boycott explained that Robinson was injured. Next over, retrieving yet another ball from the same spot, the spectator enquired why Cope wasn't bowling. Again Boycott took time out to explain, patiently and politely, that the bowler was injured. When the same thing happened again a few overs later, Boycott told the man that he would speak to him at close of play and explain everything.

Thus at stumps Geoffrey Boycott walked across to the spectator and patiently explained his tactics during the last session of play. After ten minutes of detailed insight into his captaincy, and problems, he said to the man, 'Now, does that satisfy you?'

'All I can say is God help us if they mek thee t'captain of England,' said the spectator.

The point is Geoffrey Boycott told this joke against himself – and laughed out loud at the humour of it all.

Geoffrey Boycott retired as a player in 1986. He quickly became a successful BBC television and radio commentator and later worked for Sky. He now looks after cricket events for talkSport radio.

Raymond Illingworth –
a cricket man

In the Farsley branch of Marks & Spencer there are two large photographs of Len Hutton. One shows him playing a forcing shot off the back foot. Raymond Illingworth says he is going to bring Michael Atherton shopping so he might see the position of Hutton's feet and learn a lesson from the master. This tells you all you need know about Illingworth and the town of his birth where he has dwelt all his life. It is an up hill, down dale sort of place but it fits Raymond Illingworth like his favourite slippers. It talks cricket.

The day he learnt he was to be court martialled at Lord's, Raymond Illingworth was shopping in Farsley, where an old man stopped him and said, 'You must be regretting giving up what you did for the load of trouble you've got now.' Illingworth told him, 'I think you are right. I used to have a very happy carry-on.' And now? 'I am very depressed about what has happened. I have been fifty years in the game and nobody loves cricket more than I do. It is sad, very sad, it has to end like this,' he said.

We were sitting in the conservatory of his tucked-away, cosy house. The lawn looked like it would suit Gus Fraser. Everything about the garden and his home was neat and well-ordered. It glowed with elbow grease. The chairman of selectors was wearing an England

cricket shirt, tracksuit bottoms and carpet slippers. I have known the man for thirty years and never seen him lost for words about cricket or short of an opinion. Today he says, 'I have to be careful what I say. I suppose a lot could be *sub judice*.'

He looks forlorn, as well he might. He has always been a man of strong opinion, preferring a frank exchange of views to a duel of verbal niceties. He likes to know where he stands with people and has always solved any difference of opinion by confronting the issue and not avoiding it. It is a style which served him well as commentator, captain and player but which inevitably brought him into conflict with a cabal within the TCCB whose capacity for plotting would have given any one of them the job of chief executive to the Borgias.

Having spent a lifetime keeping one step ahead of the enemy he has now delivered himself into their hands by allowing publication of a book which, in the opinion of some, might bring the game into disrepute – whatever that means. I asked him if he didn't think he had acted unwisely. He said he had already persuaded the publisher to delay the book by a year and having once changed the contract felt unable to demand another delay. Moreover, there is little doubt he feels let down by the TCCB disciplinary committee which merely slapped Devon Malcolm's wrist for writing about Illingworth and Peter Lever as if he – Malcolm – had been the victim of cruel and insensitive management. The added insult that he might have been treated differently had he been

a white bowler was retracted, but that is not to say forgotten by the victims.

'I always said I reserved the right to reply to Devon. My own view is that if the TCCB had dealt with Devon properly that would have been the end. As it is the entire issue has festered away,' he said. When he talks about Malcolm there is no anger. Rather he is sorrowful that he couldn't persuade a better performance from the bowler. He admits failure but points out he wasn't the only one. Prior to going to South Africa, Malcolm's thirty-four Tests had been spread over seven years and fourteen different series. In that time Messrs Dexter, Stewart, Fletcher, Gooch, Lamb, Gower and Atherton, as well as Illingworth, tried in vain to make him a consistent bowler of Test class.

I asked Illingworth why he bothered to pick a cricketer with such obvious deficiencies. 'Because he has pace. He was the first player I told he was going to South Africa. Informed him well before the others. Tried to get him in the right frame of mind. He was beaming, happy at the thought of meeting Nelson Mandela.' What went wrong? 'Didn't seem to want to listen. We couldn't get through to him, no matter what we tried.' What Illingworth and Lever were trying to persuade him to do was not a radical change of action. They were endeavouring to persuade him to follow through on a straight line rather than falling away to cover when he delivered. They were up against a brick wall.

The consequence of Malcolm's inconsistency led to the débâcle in Cape Town when England lost the Test

and the series. Illingworth told him, 'You bowled crap and probably cost us the Test match.' If Malcolm and his supporters cannot accept the truth of at least the first part of that statement they must be living in a different world from the rest of us who believe Illingworth was understating the case.

Malcolm looms large in the coming disciplinary hearing but other remarks Illingworth made in the book are also causing concern and will be added to the charge sheet. It appears he has broken the omerta practised by selection committees. I searched in vain for startling or compromising revelations and found none. There are tough-minded assertions about cricket and the way it is run and played but these are opinions worth listening to and considering. A major problem with the TCCB is the culture of secrecy surrounding decisions made at Lord's. If Illingworth is to be disciplined for speaking his mind, what charge might be brought against people who, although accountable to the rest of us, say nothing? The only conclusion to be made about secretive people in public places is they must have something to hide. What they seem to forget is it's our game not theirs.

I asked Raymond Illingworth if he felt like resigning. 'Of course I did. Then I went to Old Trafford for the one-day international and was overwhelmed by the kindness of people who came up to me and begged me not to walk away. Then there were the phone calls of support from people in high places, people who might surprise you,' he said. I didn't waste time asking who they might be.

'The real effect of what has happened is that it has made me disenchanted with the game for the first time. When I finish, whether that be sooner or later, I want nothing more to do with cricket,' he said. What about commentating? 'Maybe, but I want nothing more to do with the game in an official capacity as an administrator. That is a big thing for me to say because the game has been my life,' he said.

When he departs the England team, will it be in a better state than it was two years ago? 'I think so. What we've done is we've stopped losing matches too easily. We have some tough competitors in the team now. But what people must understand is there is no problem in picking a team. The problem lies in having a system which does not produce sufficient class cricketers to choose from.

'There has been a lot of soft cricket played in the past ten years. Every match in the County Championship should be competitive, like a Test match. It's not. For half a season most teams have nothing to play for. We should split the championship into two divisions and have two up and two down. There should be eighteen cricket academies throughout the land – one in every county – and a national academy based abroad, somewhere like Zimbabwe, so our best young players can go there for winter coaching. We should play on uncovered wickets and have our Test players contracted to the Board like they do in South Africa and Australia.

'South Africa is a remarkable example of what can be done with imagination and proper planning. Any

team going to play in South Africa will struggle to beat them and I don't care who they are. What is particularly impressive about their system is the way Ali Bacher operates as chief executive. You want anything doing, you tell Ali and five minutes later it's done. I could work with that system. Perfect,' he said. There was a wistful smile on his face as he contemplated a world without committees, sub-committees, working parties and the like.

As we were parting I complimented him on the condition of his lawn. 'I could make a Test wicket, you know. I understand a lot about preparation and the like. When I was a kid at Farsley I used to spend hours pushing the roller up and down the wicket, listening to the old players talking about turf and cricketers. Taught me a lot. They're grumbling nowadays about the state of the wicket at Farsley and I've told the players they've got to do their share of heavy rolling. But they don't want to do it nowadays. I don't understand,' he said.

It is sad Raymond Illingworth's love affair with English cricket will end in divorce. His consolation is knowing he has made a far more significant contribution to the game than any of his accusers, not to mention those who will sit in judgement and never mind the ones who plotted against him, both at Lord's and in the media.

There are far more important problems for the TCCB to solve than a row between the manager and one of his players or the settling of petty grievances. As Illingworth says, 'We are never going to get anywhere by squabbling. That is not the way to do it. We are simply

reducing our chances of success.' I ask him if he is a sadder but wiser man.

'Sadder, certainly,' he said.

June 1996

Raymond Illingworth's views regarding the need for two divisions in the County Championship came to fruition in the 2000 season – nine counties play in each division, with a three up three down promotion and relegation system. During the summer months, the former England and Yorkshire manager and England and Leicestershire captain can still be found mowing the grass, driving the roller and marking the pitches at his beloved Farsley ground.

DARREN GOUGH – YOUNG PRETENDER WITH THE FAST-BOWLING WORLD AT HIS FEET

I F things go according to plan and Darren Gough has a long and illustrious career bowling fast for Yorkshire and England, future biographers might like to know of a conversation that took place at Shipley golf course on Monday, 11 July 1994, when a four ball including young Master Gough encountered another four ball captained by Frederick Sewards Trueman.

'Now then, young man, who told you to bowl that rubbish at the New Zealanders in the second innings?' said Mr Trueman, who is not renowned for beating about the bush.

'I was trying to blast them out,' said Darren Gough.

'Blast them out, blast them out,' said Mr Trueman, shaking his head at such heresy. 'Your job is to bowl them out. In future don't listen to them. I'll tell you what to do.'

Their encounter was poignant because it was the old monarch meeting the young pretender. It might yet prove significant because Darren Gough is good at taking advice from people who know what they are talking about. Midway through last season [1994] he was not a happy cricketer. He was uncertain about his future, confused about what kind of bowler he should

be. He had the sublime ability to bowl fast but lacked the confidence to let himself go.

'I was in two minds. I wanted to bowl fast but I was frightened of going for eight an over,' he recalled. Gough was bowling against Hampshire's Shaun Udal, who had struck him for four, when Richie Richardson took him on one side. The West Indian captain nodded in the direction of Udal. 'I wouldn't let a batsman like him hit me for four,' he said.

'What would you do?' said Darren Gough.

'I'd let him have it,' said Richardson. And Gough did.

He said, 'It's one thing if a team-mate tries to gee you up to go flat out. It's quite another if the captain of the West Indies tells you he thinks you can bowl fast. He's got to be *the* expert on the subject, hasn't he?' Richardson, who is having a wretched time in Yorkshire, might find some consolation in Gough's gratitude. He will also receive the nation's thanks if the fast bowler becomes the cutting edge of England's attack, the sword of our ambition for the next decade or so.

There is a lot riding on Darren Gough's future. What he showed in his Test debut was not simply the ability to bowl fast or cleave about him to good effect with the bat, but an exuberance and a joy at being young and fit and playing cricket for a living that was infectious enough to engage even the most jaded observer. There was such energy and pleasure in all he did that you might have been persuaded he was doing it for fun and not for a living. The last person I saw play like that was Ian Botham. Not surprisingly, the great all-rounder is

Darren Gough

one of Gough's heroes and the reason he decided on a career in cricket.

He was born in Monk Bretton, just outside Barnsley, the same village that produced Martyn Moxon. He had trials with Rotherham United as a vigorous midfielder but decided he would rather play cricket for Yorkshire. He played at Barnsley under the keen and critical eye of the Yorkshire cricket manager Steve Oldham. Gough made his debut for his county when he was nineteen. He played at Lord's, bowled well and then didn't play until the last match of the season because of injury, one of those stress conditions to his back that are sadly commonplace nowadays in young athletes required to do too much too soon.

Although his injury meant he couldn't bowl, Gough could hold a bat, so Oldham had him going in first wicket down for Barnsley. He did well, scored a century or two and developed the talent we saw when scoring 60 odd against the New Zealand bowlers at Old Trafford. Oldham believes he could develop into a genuine all-rounder. Significantly, Gough's heroes – Botham, Sir Richard Hadlee and Malcolm Marshall – are quick bowlers who could bat a bit.

Steve Oldham has never doubted Gough's ability. I remember him telling me about the boy before he made his debut in the Yorkshire team. 'I've got a gem at Barnsley. He'll go all the way,' is what he said. Oldham is about to be proved right but would have preferred the England selectors to have waited a season or two.

'I don't think he's quite ready as a Test player yet.

He has all the ability in the world but he's still learning how to harness it to the best effect. I was watching him bowl at the Kiwis in the second innings, pitching short, trying to knock their heads off, and I nearly got on the phone to the England dressing-room to tell him to stop bowling like a prat,' said Oldham.

'His trouble is he has so much natural talent he doesn't know what to do with it. We haven't coached him at all, not in the sense of showing him how to bowl. When he came to us he could bowl outswing, off-cutters, yorkers. What we have tried to do, and what he has still to learn, is to bowl it where it counts. That's what the great strike bowlers do.'

Gough accepts the criticism but says, given a pitch with a bit of bounce in it, any fast bowler worth his reputation would find it difficult to resist banging the ball in at the batsman's rib cage.

Was he nervous in his first Test match? 'Not when I was bowling,' he replied. 'But when it came to batting, I had butterflies. First ball hit me in the ribs. Still got the bruise. Gave me an excuse to give their bowlers one or two when they batted. Not that I need an excuse. I'm not a member of the fast bowlers' club that says you don't bowl short at other fast bowlers. Do you think if I don't bowl short at Curtly he's going to let me off? Not likely.

'I'm half a yard quicker now than I was last season. I'm taking my career much more seriously than I did before. Anna, my wife, pointed out that if I wanted to reach the top I had to work at it. I'd always had the

problem of putting on weight [Oldham remembers that, when he came to Barnsley, he was a 'fat little bugger']. Anna started me off on diet and exercise. I now do specialised training on the muscles I need to bowl fast.'

He says he is now addicted to training. He stands 5ft 11ins, weighs 12st 8 lbs. He is broad-shouldered, deep-chested and blessed with strong legs. He has the physical attributes required to meet the strains and stresses caused by bowling fast. But does he possess that extra something, that magic ingredient required to make the jump from county to international cricket? Steve Oldham has no doubt. 'He's a diamond. Every hurdle we put in his way, he cleared it with style. I think he's eighteen months away from being a genuine Test bowler but what will carry him through, what will bring him triumph, is his wonderful enthusiasm.

'He responds to circumstances. When he was a bairn at Barnsley, there was one game where he was a bit listless, just turning his arm over, when a very attractive blonde girl came and sat in the pavilion. Darren saw her and started showing off. Very soon there were stumps flying all over the place.

'He's special now and when he gets some wool on his back he'll be something to reckon with. How quick is he? Major league. He puts 'em on their arse. He'll get quicker, too.'

A lot has happened to Darren Gough in the four short years he has been a professional cricketer. In 1991 *Wisden* informed him he had not lived up to his early promise. He was twenty-one at the time. A year later

he was so unhappy with his situation at Yorkshire that he seriously considered leaving the county. Not too long ago he suffered the nickname 'Guzzler'. Nowadays he's called 'Dazzler'.

Today he contemplates his first Test match at Lord's with judges as good as Raymond Illingworth and Richie Benaud convinced he is the bowler we have been searching for over long and fruitless years. Benaud reckons that if we could find another bowler of Gough's pace, we would go to Australia in November with a better chance of winning the Ashes than in many a long year.

He is also crucial to the revival of his county. It will be Gough, White, Michael Vaughan and the other young players, some as yet untried, who will carry the burden in the next decade. Gough feels that at present they are letting Martyn Moxon and Steve Oldham down. 'That hurts because they're two great guys who give young players like myself every chance,' he said.

It could be Gough's destiny not just to repay that debt but to be the player around whom the future of both his county and country might be decided. It is an awesome proposition but if achieved would earn Gough a level of fame and riches beyond his imagining. He appears to have the lot, enough talent, good looks and personality to make me wish I had shares in him. He gets fan mail from girls whose interest in cricket is not one reflected in *Wisden*. The marketing men are hovering.

He won't have a problem selling the new persona, but can he handle living with it? The signs are encouraging. Gough sat at Harrogate a few days ago holding his new

England helmet, his fingers tracing the outline of the three lions. 'I always wanted one of these,' he said.

I said it was good to see a player getting such enjoyment out of playing Test cricket. 'Oh I was determined to go out there and have a good time,' Gough responded.

'Why?' I asked.

'Well, because it might not happen again. They might not pick me next time,' he said. He meant it as well. He'll do.

October 1994

The ebullient personality of Darren Gough has made him one of England's most charismatic cricketers. His prowess as a fast bowler has given the England attack a real cutting edge; for example, he shared the new ball with Andrew Caddick in each Test of the series against the West Indies in 2000, the first time the same pair had opened the bowling throughout a series since Trueman and Statham did so versus South Africa in 1960. In 2001, Gough became the eighth England bowler to take 200 Test wickets.

ENGLAND

Tony Greig – the
anti-establishment man

Tony Greig is a purposeful man. When he strides across a room for an appointment you half expect him to break into a run and bowl a bouncer. The thatch of blond hair has been harvested by time – in other words he is a bit thin on top – but the rest is as it was. He has not shrunk any, he is still 6ft 7ins, broad-shouldered and athletic. A big man, and I would guess that not many have volunteered to throw a punch at him. I only mention this because many people would dearly love to take a swing at Tony Greig. When I told a friend of mine who I was going to interview, he said, 'Talking to traitors now.'

When, as captain of England, he threw his hand in with Kerry Packer and World Series cricket, he was denounced and reviled. The fans forgive and forget and nowadays he is given a cordial reception whenever he visits England. The establishment take longer to heal their wounds.

There are some at Lord's who cold-shoulder him; he is still waiting for news that he has been given honorary membership of the MCC like every other captain of England before and after him. He is not holding his breath.

Attempting to explain what he saw as Greig's dis-loyalty by signing with Packer, the cricket correspondent of *The Times* wrote in 1977: 'What has to be

remembered, of course, is that he is an Englishman not by birth or upbringing, but only by adoption. It is not the same thing as being English through and through.'

What, I wonder, would the writer say about the English 'through and through' cricketers who went on rebel tours to South Africa and included in their numbers one or two captains of England? When put to the test, their loyalty depended not upon birthright but the lure of the rand. Similarly, Greig, and others, were bought by the Aussie dollar.

What was never in doubt was Greig's determination on the field of play to make England the best cricket team in the world. He did not succeed but what he did do was hand over to Michael Brearley a much better team than the one he inherited from Mike Denness.

In 1977 Brearley's team won the Ashes. *The Times* wrote a leader in celebration of the event and gave Greig the credit. It said: 'He took over a side being compared with the very worst in England's cricketing history, made its members believe in their individual and collective abilities, and by his own flamboyant, perhaps over-aggressive example, instilled confidence into a team that had become accustomed to losing.'

In other words, just the kind of chap we want right now to rejuvenate our cricket team. In any shortlist of candidates approved by the TCCB, Greig's application to be our next chairman of selectors would be slightly ahead of Pol Pot and only just behind Geoffrey Boycott. Not that he is inclined to apply.

At present he works for Kerry Packer's 9 Television

Network as the sales director for satellite television. Packer looks after his own. He also fronts up the Channel 9 television presentation of cricket, and very good he is at it too, being knowledgeable, provocative and outspoken. He does not allow his audience in Australia to forget that he was once captain of England and on our side in any Ashes encounter. Such loyalty has left him a forlorn figure during this season's débâcle.

'A nightmare' is how he describes it. 'For the first time this year, I gave up. I never threw the towel in when I was playing but watching England over the past few months has left me speechless. Worst of all, my fellow commentators are feeling sorry for me. They've stopped having a go at me for supporting England because they've seen how hopeless the situation is. Fifteen years of creating a commentating style undermined by a single series.'

He shakes his head in sorrow. 'When I took over the captaincy we were struggling, Lillee and Thomson were knocking us over. I wanted someone to stick there, someone with guts and a good technique. I spoke to the old pros on the county circuit, people like Bob Cottam, and asked them who was the person they found most difficult to get out. They all said David Steele.

'I went to the selectors and said I wanted Steele in my side. They thought I'd gone bloody mad. But we picked him and he did the job for us,' he said.

Steele, for twelve seasons an ordinary county pro, found himself nominated as one of *Wisden*'s five

cricketers of the year. He became a national hero. The next season Tony Greig made his famous prediction that his team would make the visiting West Indians 'grovel'. Roberts, Holding and Daniel took up the challenge in such a manner as to question the resolve of all but the stoutest hearts.

'We were playing on a road at Old Trafford and I wanted a couple of tough old bastards to go out there and face up to the quicks,' said Greig. He persuaded the selectors to recall Close and Edrich. In England's second innings they were battered by a sustained assault of fast, short-pitched bowling which Close, in typical fashion, chose to play with his chest. It was glorious but it was futile. England lost. Close and Edrich were dropped for the next Test.

'The point I'm making is that Alec Bedser, who was then the chairman of selectors, would accommodate me if I felt strongly about picking a player,' Greig continued. 'But more than that, I was the person who talked to the press. Not the chairman of selectors, but the team manager. So in that respect I was accountable.

'The first thing Michael Atherton should do is insist on being the only person in the England set-up to speak to the press. The captain should give a press conference every night after play no matter what the situation. If he feels uncomfortable with it then find someone to appear who isn't. You have to establish a proper relationship with the media.

'I once kicked out a senior England player who came to one press conference in his new career as a journalist.

He was drunk. I told him, "I'm sober and I'm here to talk sensibly to you. You're drunk. I suggest you leave and come back when you're capable of doing your job." He left and wrote me an apology.

'Alec Bedser wrote a piece the other day pointing out that he was the only chairman of selectors for the past thirty-eight years who didn't go to Cambridge University. It was a fair point.

'Who are these people running England's cricket? At least when Gubby Allen was at Lord's you knew where you were, but who's in charge now, who's pulling the strings – A.C. Smith, Wheatley, Doug Insole? What the chairmen of the counties should demand is that people are made accountable for their actions. Who, for instance, was in favour of giving Fletcher a five-year contract?

'If M.J.K. Smith gets Dexter's job, who are the people promoting him? So often it seems that the counties are merely rubber-stamping decisions taken by some TCCB committee.

'I'm worried about the idea of a supremo. If we went that way, Boycott would be the ideal man. He knows so much about the game and he's developed into a first-class communicator.'

Greig favours three or four selectors. 'Boycott, Brearley, Illingworth, Fletcher even. Then I'd appoint a coach, but this would be the captain's choice. If Atherton wanted Boycott then Geoff would have the job so long as Atherton was captain.

'But in the end we have to look at what's wrong, at

the foundations of English cricket. What World Series cricket did for Australian cricket was to show how strong commercial influences could work to the benefit of the game and the players. The best players, the Test cricketers, have benefited the most.

'The message to the rest of the players is clear: either graduate to Test cricket standard or make way for someone else who might. English cricketers ought to be put to the same examination.

'You've got to make the game more exciting, more glamorous. In Australia we did this through the one-day, day-night games. To the purists who denounce it as being tacky I would only say it's like eating hamburgers and then graduating to dining in French restaurants. In other words, the one-day leads a new audience to Test cricket.

'I'd get rid of all the present one-day competitions in England. If the Sunday League survived I would like to see the TCCB issue a directive saying that each county side must contain four or five players chosen from local clubs.

'This would give the chance to the good club player to test himself at a higher level. I'd also have a fifteen-match one-day triangular tournament, like we have in Australia,' he said.

'I think there is a real crisis in English cricket. Things won't change until we target and eliminate the people responsible for the current state of affairs. They have created a bloody almighty mess. The trouble is the real villains don't show their heads. Until they are identified

and made accountable for their actions, things won't change for the better.'

'What are the chances of radical change?' I asked.

'About the same chance you and I have of flying to the moon,' said Tony Greig.

August 1993

Tony Greig lives in Australia where he is a leading commentator on international cricket.

MIKE GATTING – AN
APPETITE FOR THE GAME

WHEN he came in the restaurant he looked trim, fit and clear-eyed, like a contender. In fact, he had just been told that he wasn't in the tour party to the West Indies (which he expected), nor had he been chosen to lead the A team to South Africa (which he thought he might). So, Mike Gatting, what are your comments, please? He shrugged his shoulders.

'The door is shut on my Test career. I suppose that's what it means,' he said. Disappointed? 'Of course. I love playing for England. Goochie had some of his best years for England after he started going grey. Why shouldn't me and Gower do the same?

'On the other hand, it will be good to have a winter in England. I don't think the family will mind me being home for Christmas. I've had fifteen years, good years at that, with England. So I can't complain,' he said.

What will you do? 'Don't know. Look around. I used to be a plumber you know. Might take that up again.' You used to be what? 'Well, a plumber's mate really. When I was at school I used to work with this plumber. Learned a lot about it. It's all about organisation really. Might set myself up doing central-heating systems and the like.'

He likes organising things, Mike Gatting. He thinks captaincy is about organising players into the right place

Mike Gatting

at the right time and in the right frame of mind. 'It will be a trying time for Mike Atherton in the West Indies. First of all, the quicks will be after him. The way they operate is seek and destroy the captain and demolish the side's confidence. He had better get used to the fact that he is not going to get many pitched in his own half.

'Then he has to convince the team that they are on tour playing cricket and not on holiday. That's a problem with every touring party, but it's a particular problem in the Windies where it seems like carnival time wherever you go. Sometimes it's difficult to organise net practice and very easy for players to drift off and not concentrate on the job in hand.

'I think they have been very brave picking a young side. I do think it might have been wiser to have taken at least one experienced player but there is no doubt that playing the West Indian pace bowlers is a job for quick eyes and lightning reflexes. If I was to offer any advice to Mike it would be to talk to his team, get them to think about the way they do things. It seems self-evident to say that different players need a different approach, but not every captain understands that.

'When I had Ian Botham in the team and we won the Ashes in Australia, he made a significant contribution because I think I handled him the right way. I didn't insist that he have nets every day or do all the physical training. I'm glad they've picked Chris Lewis. He bowled well in India without much luck. Had an unhappy series against Australia and got dropped. He needs talking to . . . understanding, then see him go.'

Michael Gatting learned in a tough school. The Middlesex record through the 1980s and 1990s is an excellent one with only the odd blip. It was achieved by good cricketers being well led. That much is certainly true of the present team, who have finished the season as the champion county.

Gatting is at home with players such as Emburey, Fraser and Desmond Haynes. He admires the way they think about the game, talk about it. 'After a day's play we try to get all the players to sit down and talk about the game. We're looking for awareness, understanding. There's a tendency for some of the young players in county cricket to finish playing, put the gear on and go out dancing. That's sad,' he said.

What about one or two of the younger players in the Middlesex team who have a reputation for being difficult or temperamental? Ramprakash for instance. 'He has never tried it on with me.' Next question. What about Tufnell? He thought carefully about this one. 'He knows where he stands with me,' he said, eventually.

It is not inconceivable that Mike Gatting might have skippered England for as long as Allan Border captained Australia. There are few who doubt he is England's best county captain. He was the last England captain to win the Ashes in Australia, or anywhere else for that matter. The reason he did not emulate Border is the much-discussed incident at Faisalabad where he had a row with the Pakistan umpire Shakoor Rana.

'Worst mistake of my life. What I did was wrong in that you must never argue with an umpire. I think I

should have come home. Perhaps the team should have pulled out. Something needed to be done. A lot was going on and nothing was being done about it.' What was going on? He smiled, sadly. 'I'm not going to say any more about it. I'd only get into more trouble. One day the truth will be told.'

Scyld Berry, the experienced cricket correspondent of the *Sunday Telegraph*, covered the tour and had no doubt what was happening. He wrote: 'The Faisalabad Affair has been almost buried, if not covered up, so that the essential truth of it has not been widely grasped. Beyond reasonable doubt the England players were right in thinking that the Test series was "fixed" by a Pakistan regime which has mercifully moved on. Pressure, direct and indirect, was put on the umpires to bring about a Pakistan victory in the first Test and to halt England in the second at Faisalabad. When Gatting exploded . . . most human beings would have done the same as he did, following the accumulated injustices. Gatting was as good as stitched up.'

The injustice rankles still, particularly because of a further demonstration of Rana's seedy nature. A year later the umpire, who was writing a book about the incident, turned up at Worcester, where Middlesex were playing, accompanied by a newspaper photographer.

'He was tapping on the window of my car saying he wanted to talk to me, to explain things. All the time the photographer was snapping away. A stunt. I didn't react. One day I'll give my version of events,' said Gatting.

Rana might be a clown, and worse, but he did for the captain of England. There is little doubt that when Gatting was deposed for behaving irresponsibly in inviting female company to his hotel room for a drink, the hierarchy had more on its mind than a mere dalliance with a barmaid. Gatting has no doubt. 'It was a back-dated punishment,' he said.

That led to Gatting going to South Africa. It might have made him a lot of money but it did little for his public relations. 'I felt left out and let down by the England set-up. Was I condemned to county cricket for the rest of my life? That uncertainty pushed me to South Africa.

'What it taught me was to do a bit of homework before jumping into a volatile situation. What it also showed me was how all sides used cricket as a propaganda weapon,' he said. What he miscalculated was the kind of madness stirred by an emotive issue like South Africa. His wife received death threats. He had to employ a security firm to guard the house.

When the authorities decided to pardon the rebels the scene was set for Gatting to write a satisfying final chapter to his career. Instead, he was part of the débâcle in India and Sri Lanka and an early casualty of the hammering by the Australians.

If he ever thought the gods were against him – and he had every reason to believe so – then the message of confirmation was delivered by Shane Warne in the Old Trafford Test. His first ball to Gatting pitched way outside leg stump, turned square and took Gatting's off

bail. It announced an extraordinary new talent to Test cricket, triggered a series of events which led to a fundamental rethink of the England set-up and sealed the fate of stalwarts like Gower and Gatting.

'It's not the end of my cricket career. I might not play for England again but I am certainly going to go on playing for Middlesex. I reckon I have three to four more years in me. I still have an appetite for cricket. Even if I wasn't captain, I would play on as a member of the team if they wanted me. After that? Wouldn't mind a job as coach. Like to put something more back into the game,' he said.

Coming from someone else it sounds like a cliché. From Mike Gatting it is a statement of intent. It is good news for Middlesex that he is not disenchanted with the game. It gives the county a guarantee that for a few more years any victory for the opposition will be gained only over the dead body of Mike Gatting.

For all the tumult of his career, he has few regrets. 'What I would like to have done was play in that period of time when Compo and Edrich were at Lord's and the crowds spilled over on to the grass. That would have been nice. I'd have liked to have gone to Australia on a boat as they used to. Take your time getting there. It must have been wonderful to have played in a more leisurely era,' he said.

It may be that when he finally departs there is less of a lament than accompanied Ian Botham or is likely to be heard when David Gower goes. He is not the sort of cricketer to cause an extraordinary meeting of the

MCC, nor the kind who would be comfortable sitting on stage telling anecdotes. And yet he is more durable than they, and his contribution to cricket – particularly his beloved county – is something few cricketers have achieved.

September 1993

Mike Gatting is recognised as one of the most knowledgeable coaches in England and from October 2002 will be a member of the MCC Committee.

DAVID GOWER – TIME
TO SPARE

THE man on the gate asked what I was doing. When I told him I had come to interview David Gower he said, 'Make sure you write something nice about him.'

The lady in the tearoom had much the same advice. A man called Brian, jumpy as a ferret, sought me out, anxious that the interview would not dwell too much on the possibility that Gower might be thinking of retiring after this season.

'Our job is to get him back in the England side, then on the tour of the West Indies. He needs to be encouraged to have positive thoughts,' he said. I asked him if, perchance, he was related to Donald Trelford. He said he wasn't. He was a retired businessman who had volunteered to help Gower by looking after his mental welfare. I inspected him for cracks. He seemed all right, which is remarkable considering that cricket is littered with gibbering wrecks of people who have tried to fathom what goes on in Gower's head.

The public concern for Gower is as touching as it is extraordinary. Of the athletes I have known, only George Best aroused the same emotions in people and even he, in his pomp, would have been hard pushed to fill City Hall, Westminster, with people demanding that Tommy Docherty stop playing silly sods with his career.

Apart from blessed talent the two men have one other thing in common. It is that once you start asking them to explain themselves the mystery deepens. I had the first evidence of the enigmatic part of Gower's personality at the beginning of his career. It was 1975 and his first season with Leicestershire. I was having a talk with Ray Illingworth, then captain of the county, about new talent and he said, 'I've a young boy in my team who will one day play for England. In all my years in cricket I've not seen many who can time a ball like this lad.'

This was worth noting because Illingworth is as good a judge of a cricketer as ever lived. What is more, he doesn't often wax lyrical. He added, 'His name is David Gower. He'll go all the way, providing he wants to.' That note of caution was the earliest indication of the problem Gower has always had of convincing people that he possessed the depth of will to underpin his matchless talent.

Illingworth's caution was probably due to an incident early in Gower's career when he turned up for a game wearing odd shoes, one brown, the other black. This provoked a telling off from Illingworth and a lecture on the importance of always being smart and well turned out.

The captain was seated at breakfast on the morning of the next match when Gower strode into the dining-room dressed in dark blue dinner suit, bow tie and highly polished black shoes. Illingworth looked aghast at his player and said, 'Bloody hell, Gower, have you just come in?'

More than 8,000 Test runs and countless japes later, Illingworth's protégé sits in the Hampshire dressing-room achieving the impossible, namely, looking elegant in a tracksuit. He seems happy and at ease.

Mark Nicholas says that during the past few weeks Gower has been as relaxed and content as he has ever known him to be. Why? Has he been told to ready himself for a trip to the West Indies? Alternatively, has he decided that this is his last season and is he smiling at the prospect of not having to play county cricket seven days a week? Perhaps he has concluded that he owes Hampshire something, and is trying even harder to support Nicholas and his team.

We are here to find out. First the question of a return to the England team. 'Earlier in the season I thought I had a real chance. I made 153 against Notts and felt good. Then I cracked my rib. End of story. After the reshuffle in the Test team I think my chances of being recalled have lessened.

'Let's be frank, I don't want to bat at number seven for England. Being positive, I suppose you could argue that if there was one reshuffle there could be another. If there is I could be in with a chance. I am in the lucky position of having so many people taking up the case on my behalf. Is that an added pressure to do well? Maybe, but it's much more pleasant than having people gunning for you.

'Will I retire if I don't get picked for the Windies? I wouldn't rule it out. It's the usual conundrum, when to go. The first time it was suggested I might retire was in

1986. We were touring Australia, I had lost the captaincy and was feeling low and the press started speculating I might leave the game. A trifle premature, I thought. I wasn't even thirty. Now I'm thirty-six and the prospect of retirement is obviously more real.

'I suppose if county cricket was designed differently I might contemplate a longer career than I do. It's no secret I don't enjoy playing cricket seven days a week. I don't like the Sunday game because of its artificiality. What would suit me would be one four-day game every two weeks,' he said. I must have looked surprised. 'All right, make that one four-day game a week and no Sunday games,' he said.

'In any event, I don't want to drag out the end. I don't want my career to die a dismal death. Ideally, I'd like to go out in a Test match or a NatWest final. Something meaningful. Seems unlikely. I wonder if I could persuade Ted [Dexter, chairman of England selectors] to arrange to pick me for the last Test to make my grand exit. What do you think?'

I said the current England selectors were not renowned for flamboyant gestures. 'Perhaps we could persuade the MCC to invent some centenary game, or we might have a special farewell match at Lord's for the David Gower Relief Fund. Seriously, though, it doesn't happen like that, does it? I think you wake up one morning and say, "Well, that's it. That's life. Time to go."'

We were talking before Ian Botham made his exit. I imagine that his departure from the scene would be regarded as another indication to Gower that this season

might well be his last. Botham is a soulmate, someone who, like Gower, has no difficulty in being persuaded that while cricket is a wonderful and uplifting occupation there are other things in life as intoxicating, perhaps more so.

With his departure and Allan Lamb no longer an England player, Gower must feel increasingly that he might be overstaying his welcome. The three of them played their cricket the same way and shared a distaste for the squat-thrust and push-up regime of the England team of recent years. Gower says in his autobiography that he would like the words 'Fun, style and excellence' as his epitaph. It was a philosophy he lived by. It won him a million friends but in the end it did for him.

When did he realise that his philosophy was also his undoing? 'Tiger Moth. Need I say more? When I sat down in a room afterwards with Gooch and Stewart and talked about the meaning of life and they put to me their disenchantment and I did the same, I realised that this was the end of the road.

'There is still some of the atmosphere of that meeting hanging in the air. I feel that I haven't been picked for England on occasions for the sake of a few runs at the right time, whereas my record and reputation as a Test player has not been taken into account. It makes you think when many good judges say you should have played more. But I don't like moaning. Let's just say that when you introduce a regimen, bravado disappears,' he said.

What he likes about Hampshire is that under the

tolerant and kindly eye of Mark Nicholas his vagaries have been accommodated. Does he owe them a debt? 'I don't think I do. The club has been understanding and I am grateful but I think I've made a contribution in the last three years. Not just statistics either. I think I've played my part in the dressing-room, trying to keep part of it sane.'

So will he be there next season or will he be in a commentary box with his sparring partner, Geoffrey Boycott, the man who once said that the perfect player would have Gower's talent and Boycott's brain? Gower replied to this theory by agreeing that while he might have scored more Test runs, he would not have ended up with as many friends.

When he goes he will make many people very sad. All of us will have special memories. My own is Sydney in the tour of 1990–91 and Gower playing an innings of incomparable charm and beauty. It might be, of course, that between now and the end of the season he will do enough to convince the selectors that they must take him to the West Indies. I wonder. Although he denies it, I have the feeling that Gower has already made up his mind.

Before our interview, I watched him bat against Worcestershire. He scored 30 odd in his inimitable manner before touching a lifter to slip. When he came in he signed autographs patiently and willingly. During our talk he was approached and interrupted many times, sometimes with foolish requests. Never once was he less than courteous and obliging. I was reminded, not for

the first time, that I have always been as impressed by Gower's manners as I have by his talent.

Talking to him the other day I was made aware, for the first time, that I have witnessed all of Gower's career in cricket, from Illingworth and the first predictions of glory to Portsmouth and the first intimations of retirement. When I tell my grandchildren about David Gower, I will say that apart from the obvious glories of his batting, what I was most grateful for was that he never gave me cause to be concerned about or ashamed of the game of cricket.

In everything he did, on and off the field, he embodied the qualities of the greatest of games. And when he chooses the moment and the setting of his leaving, we can be sure it will be done in great style, with perfect timing.

July 1993

David Gower has developed a successful career on television, as a commentator for Sky Sports and on a long-running BBC sports panel game. An accomplished after-dinner speaker, he remains one of the most courteous and well mannered of cricketers.

Graham Gooch – a lasting monument

I JOURNEYED to Cambridge on a chirruping, blossoming spring day and saw Graham Gooch give a masterclass to the eager young pups of the Combined Universities, his bat echoing like a bass gong around Fenner's. He scored a century.

Two days later at Chelmsford against Worcestershire he almost scored another. His last three trips to the crease have yielded 317 first-class runs. He might have finished with Test cricket but no one should doubt his determination to defend his reputation as our best batsman.

Anyone who watched Gooch on the last tour of Australia could be in no doubt that he was right to announce his retirement. It was, as he admits, a tour too far. Nonetheless, I have no doubt that there will come a moment during the summer with Ambrose and Walsh on the rampage when we would all feel much better with Gooch at the crease, unflinching, resolute and proven in the heat of battle.

The circumstances leading to Gooch's retirement had nothing to do with a fraying of technique or nerve, nor lack of appetite for the encounter. In the end, his body told him to quit. There was a time in cricket's history when Gooch, at forty-two with twenty-two seasons behind him, might still have been a force in the inter-

national game. That he has lasted this long as the game became faster, fitter and younger is a tribute to his determined and relentless pursuit of excellence.

In a new book about his life written along with the excellent Frank Keating, Gooch says that when he came into the pavilion at Perth having played his last Test match, he was content with the thought he could always look in the mirror and say, 'If I did nothing else, I know I always did my best.'

If you find the statement simplistic, even mawkish, then you fail to understand the man. Gooch believes in the solid virtues of hard work and dedication. This is a man who carries dumb-bells in his suitcase to exercise with, who would think nothing of running a few miles from hotel to ground and back again, who in the chaos of a dressing-room had his own controlled space with everything in its place and in apple-pie order. He left nothing to chance.

If this meticulous preparation was the cornerstone of his success, it was also one of the reasons why his public reputation was of a dour, even dull, man. In the famous dispute with David Gower, Gooch was cast as the Black Knight and it was Gower who rode the white charger, the sunlight dappling his golden hair.

With his sloping shoulders and world-weary manner, Gooch was easy meat for the media whenever they felt like blaming body language for the problems of our cricket team; nor did he help himself. He has always been wary about opening his mouth in public. In the book he recalls an early incident in the Essex dressing-

Graham Gooch

room when, as he sat in the corner trying to avoid the attention of the captain, 'Tonker' Taylor, Keith Fletcher nodded over in his direction and said, 'Does it talk?'

Well it does, and very fluently when it has to, as we shall soon discover. But Gooch is not a soundbite cricketer. He doesn't feel the need to underline his achievements with words, preferring people to make up their own minds about what they have witnessed.

This was most famously demonstrated after he had scored 333 runs against the Indians. We asked how did he feel and waited, pencils poised, to report the torrent of words from a man who had just scored a triple century in a Test match. 'All right, I suppose,' said Graham Gooch.

But he is not a sourpuss – quite the opposite. He has a sly, but deep, sense of humour. He is, as Keating observes, 'the most companionable of men'. After reading his book I am also prepared to shortlist him as the most forgiving of men. What strikes you as you read this painstaking account of his life is the lack of malice, the way he sidesteps paying back old grievances.

Ted Dexter, before he became chairman of selectors, once wrote that Gooch's captaincy had the effect on him of 'a slap in the face with a cold fish'. All Gooch has to say about that insult is to observe that Mr Dexter is entitled to his opinion.

Indeed, the book is so short on hair-raising, headline-making, sensational revelation that an interview published the day I met him at Fenner's concentrated on the break-up of his marriage and asked the question, 'Is

he the sort of man who needs a woman to look after him?'

We sat at Fenner's on a bench, near the wall at the back of the pavilion. Earlier I had watched him bowl, an unexpected pleasure brought about by Neil Williams pulling a hamstring and Gooch, ever the willing work-horse, taking over in an emergency. After every over, as he trudged away to his position in the deep, slope-shouldered, slightly knock-kneed, head bowed, he looked for all the world like a ploughman returning home after a back-breaking day in the fields. At such moments you would have a hard job convincing the stranger to the game that Gooch was one of the most glorious batsmen of modern times, someone who could make even the best bowlers seem accommodating; nor would it prepare you for when you met him – the attractive mien, the frank and humorous blue-green eyes, the agreeable, easy manner.

I asked him if he had been tempted when writing the book to answer the critics, to rout his enemies. It had, after all, been a controversial career. The Gower affair and the Dexter observation were nothing compared to the abuse he took after the rebel tour to South Africa. The team was labelled 'Gooch's Dirty Dozen'. He tells the story that upon his return he heard a father say to his son, 'That's Graham Gooch.' The son replied, 'Dad, isn't he the man you call "the traitor"?'

Gooch said, 'I was interested in putting the record straight but not in paying back in kind. That's not my style. When I was writing the book, all I could think

about was how lucky I was to play cricket for a living and to play with and against such a good bunch of blokes. I have enjoyed the game for twenty-two years. Why get angry about that?'

He was lucky in his apprenticeship. The Essex team of his youth was a lively mixture of hard-nosed professionals including Keith Fletcher and sometimes barmy individuals such as 'Tonker' Taylor. It was Fletcher who had the most profound effect on Gooch's career. Gooch repays the debt by calling him 'a genius'. 'Tonker' Taylor, who played his cricket as if he was batting on Clacton beach, once reported umpire Cec Pepper for 'over-excessive and noisy farting'.

During his time, Gooch has seen the first-class game change almost beyond recognition. He said, 'Gone are the days when you could come on a cricket field and just swan about. There is a new athleticism in the game, there are new standards of fitness to be met. Australia was the latest example.

'They have a strength of purpose, a desire to succeed that we must learn from. Will we? Good question. We didn't alter the tour of '91 and the lesson was there then.

'What drives me mad about our cricket is the lack of consistency. We play well for one Test match and then perform like idiots in the next. I think our young cricketers have got to look inside themselves and ask how much they want the job. They have to realise that they have to do the important part themselves, that no one can hand it to them on a plate.

'They must understand that to succeed at the top level in any job involves sacrifice. Too much of our young talent is lost in a mire of mediocrity. There's a lot of dead wood in county cricket and it must be got rid of.

'In the end, it's all about self-motivation. Daley Thompson once told me that he wanted to show his rivals that he was the first to arrive for training and the last to leave. He wanted them to be aware that he was prepared to work harder than they were at being the best. People often laughed at me and my attitude towards training. But I didn't do it for fun. What I know for certain is I never saw a fitter, stronger cricketer ever become a worse cricketer,' he said. One or two of our young players who went to Australia last time should take that advice to heart.

So, in the final analysis who would he, the perfectionist, choose as the best eleven players he has played either with or against? Boycott was his favourite opening partner but he doesn't get in the team. Barry Richards and Sunil Gavaskar are the openers. Then Viv Richards, Allan Border, Javed Miandad, Ian Botham, Alan Knott, Malcolm Marshall ('the most brilliant fast bowler of my time'), Wasim Akram, Shane Warne and Curtly Ambrose.

How long will Graham Gooch remain playing for Essex? 'A couple of seasons I should think. Just so long as I enjoy it and can play to the required standard,' he said.

Then he went out to bat and face the young men from Cambridge, Oxford and Durham who were either

unborn or in nappies when he made his first-class debut.

They ran in with great vigour, the chance of bowling a legend lending them extra ambition and strength. In the end a surfeit of testosterone was not enough. The ardent young men were given a tutorial.

It was reassuring watching Graham Gooch bat on a lovely, dreamy English day. There was a beguiling serenity about the occasion, a sense of time standing still.

A new cricket season, a great player in full flow. Let it last forever. If only.

May 1995

After holding various coaching posts around the country, Graham Gooch returned to the position for which he was born, that of coach to Essex. He dabbled in the media for a while, always happy to talk about cricket, but gave the impression that he was more comfortable with players than pundits.

MICHAEL ATHERTON – A REMARKABLE ENGLISHMAN

WHEN Michael Atherton was asked what he thought about his newly published authorised biography he said he hadn't read it.

The first Jon Holmes, his agent and friend, knew about Atherton's OBE was when he read about it in the newspaper. Holmes rang to ask why Atherton hadn't told him about the honour. 'I forgot,' his client said. Holmes says both incidents reveal how much Atherton is consumed by the business of being a cricketer.

'He isn't being smart or nonchalant. When he plays cricket, particularly when he is captaining England, he is totally absorbed to the exclusion of all else,' he said.

It was revealing to hear him at his benefit dinner in London talking about the need for 'passion' in a successful team. It is not a word you associate with Michael Atherton. When you think of him, less romantic words come to mind, like cool, withdrawn, remote. We are as likely to see Atherton smoulder with passion as we are to encounter an iceberg with a smoking chimney. On the other hand, any man who can survive the ordeals he has been through with his enthusiasm as strong as ever must be either barmy or in love.

When he walks out at Old Trafford next week he is

deserving of a special ovation, not just because he is the local lad made good, or it is his benefit year, or that he has captained England more than any other player and his team are one up against the Aussies, but because he has proved himself a very remarkable Englishman with a special place in the hearts of anyone who likes to watch a battler in action.

There were early indications of his single, not to say bloody, mindedness. His mother remembers the solemn child who rarely laughed, happy in his own company, independent at a young age. At Manchester Grammar School his reliability as a cricketer was underlined by a report which noted in 1982: 'An extraordinary event took place this season; Michael Atherton played and missed.' When he was sixteen and being coached by Peter Lever, he impressed the Lancashire and England player by wanting to discuss the mental aspects of playing professional cricket.

Mark Nicholas, who captained Atherton on an A team tour in 1990, recalls a team meeting where it was suggested the best catcher in the squad should field at backward point. Atherton said, 'I'd better go there. I don't drop anything.' Nicholas recalls, 'Of course, he took a brilliant one-handed catch and gave me that "I told you so" look. He has an incredible confidence in his own ability and capabilities.'

It is true to say not everyone is as complimentary about Michael Atherton. Freddie Titmus believes he is lucky to be England captain, and a man who wrote to me the other day was apoplectic about him being

awarded the OBE. (To be fair I must report the letter was written in purple ink and some words were incomplete, having fallen off the page.) Perhaps Ray Illingworth was nearest the mark when he said that whatever people might think about Michael Atherton, one characteristic was beyond dispute: he is stubborn.

Jon Holmes agrees. 'He is the most stubborn man I have ever met. A cussed, awkward, determined character who can drive you mad in real life, and yet in the middle those characteristics make him the cricketer and leader he is. Who else but an awkward cuss, someone who refuses to bow down to conventional thinking, who loves stuffing his critics and proving them wrong, could have played that innings in South Africa? We thought the game was lost. He knew it wasn't. That's his quality.'

Atherton's innings of 185 to save the game in Johannesburg and his partnership with Jack Russell have been woven into the permanent tapestry of cricket. Illingworth thought it the greatest Test innings ever. Typically, Atherton's comment was that his best time as captain came after that innings because he was on a high and all the decisions came easily. The relationship with Illingworth was uneasy but with hindsight can probably be seen as a defining moment in Atherton's career.

There were many people – and I was one – who imagined a combination of Illingworth and Atherton to be an ideal solution to England's problems. We reasoned they shared a common philosophy and personality; peas from the same pod. We were right about that, but the

similarities made the relationship impossible: the immovable object and the irresistible force. There were differences too, and these didn't help. The generation gap between the two men was too wide to bridge. What we hadn't realised was just how big the difference was between the cricketers of Illingworth's generation and today's. Jeans, mobile phones, sunglasses, unshaven faces are the common currency of modern youth, yet certain indications to the bus-pass generation that we have gone to the dogs.

Moreover, Atherton objected to the way Illingworth conducted the business of being England boss through the media. 'I don't care what's said within four walls of the dressing-room or selection meeting,' he said, 'but that's where it must begin and end. It should not finish up on the back pages of the tabloids. I always felt that Illy was too available to the idea . . . it seemed to me he got led up the garden path on occasion.'

Atherton's own relationship with the media is interesting. He is getting better at television interviews although he can still be perverse. After defeating the Australians 3–0 in the one-day series he appeared on television looking glum. Quite rightly he was admonished by Jon Holmes, who asked him why. 'I didn't want to appear to be gloating,' he said.

His relationship with the print media is on the defensive side of wary. He has many friends in the press box with whom he enjoys convivial and trusting relationships. However, he appears not to enjoy press conferences. He feels he has been misquoted in the past so he

takes a minimalist approach to answering questions, working on the principle that if he doesn't say much he has a better chance of not being misquoted. This is wishful thinking given the imagination of some members of the fourth estate.

A group of people were discussing Atherton's attitude towards the media and wondering how they might characterise it. David Gower said, 'It's partly due to being born in Lancashire, partly due to being brought up in Manchester, partly due to being a stubborn devil but mostly it's due to being a professional cricketer confronted by pillocks with a pen.' Given the way he refuses to suffer fools at all, never mind gladly, it is remarkable Atherton has lasted as long as he has at his chosen profession. Having done so, it is possible he sees calmer waters ahead.

He is now surrounded by people he both likes and admires. Having selectors who still play the game is a huge comfort. David Graveney is a friend, David Lloyd a trusted confidant. Lord MacLaurin seems to have got a grip. The team is confident and well managed. Atherton himself is showing more confidence and flexibility as a captain.

Problems remain. His back still gives him gyp. He doesn't let on and it's not his nature to whinge, but he is quoted in the biography as saying: 'The period after my back operation in 1991 was pretty desperate. Lying there on my back one endless day after another, the thought did cross my mind it was all slipping away. Since then I've always known my days were numbered, so to speak.

Ultimately, the state of my back might have the final say in how long I play for England. I might just make the millennium. I've prepared myself for not going any further than that.'

He will always be haunted by the incident in which he was accused of tampering with the ball during a Test match. It remains a mystery. His friends might dismiss it as a storm in a teacup, but critics will always believe he should have been sacked from the captaincy and froth at the mouth when they see OBE after his name.

His own views on this and other matters, like what he really thought of Raymond Illingworth and one or two others he worked and played with, will obviously be more closely examined in his autobiography. I can't help feeling that we haven't yet seen what is inside the oyster.

June 1997

Since his retirement in 2001 Michael Atherton has become a newspaper correspondent and a television cricket commentator.

The
Australians

AUSTRALIANS — BLOOD BROTHERS

I USED to dream of going to Australia. My father told me that if he won the pools he would take me there. He never got lucky, but I did. Sadly he had died by the time I could afford the air tickets. He wanted to sit on the Hill at Sydney and give the Aussies what for. I went on his behalf and sat there for both of us thinking how he would have relished the mateyness of the Aussie spectators and their love of an argument.

My father firmly believed that Australians and Yorkshiremen were of the same tribe. Sworn enemies, yet blood brothers.

I once sat with him at Bradford in 1948 when Bradman's seemingly invincible team came nearer to defeat than at any other time on the tour.

The star of the game was Keith Miller. He won the match with his bowling and in the first innings made the highest score in grand style while the rest fooled about. I asked my father what he thought of Miller. 'I wish he played for us,' he said.

It was after seeing him play in that game that I put a photograph of Miller in my wardrobe opposite a picture of Betty Grable wearing a white swimsuit.

One day I saw my father looking at my collection of pin-ups. 'They ought to get married them two and come and live round here,' he said.

He was of the opinion that a son born of that liaison might have Miller's shoulders and Miss Grable's legs and would make a fine quick bowler.

He was not to know, and nor could I have imagined, that Keith Miller would become my friend and my guide in Australia. I first met him when we both worked for the *Daily Express* and were required to play an annual cricket match against our arch rivals, the *Daily Mail*.

Miller had little or no interest in the contest because he never enjoyed taking candy from children. However, bribed by the promise of a good pub lunch and a phone line to his bookie, he was persuaded to turn out.

It was after a liquid lunch that I happened to be standing next to my hero in the slips. He was only bothering to keep his eyes open because he had his own tic-tac man who would appear at regular intervals and signal the news from Wincanton.

Thus I was crouched as our fast bowler thundered in, while Miller stood, hands in pockets, gazing towards the pub. The batsman nicked the ball which came swiftly to my right. I was thinking about a dive when Miller swooped to his left, completed a somersault and handed me the ball, saying, 'I wonder what won that bloody race?'

When I first visited Australia in the late seventies, it was Miller who had the idea of inviting me to lunch to meet a few 'fair dinkum' Aussies who didn't mind having a beer and a yarn with a Pom. I arrived at Miller's club to find that the table consisted of Raymond Russell Lindwall, Jack Fingleton, Neil Harvey, Arthur Morris,

Alan Davidson, Bill O'Reilly and Harold Larwood. I thought I had died and gone to heaven. In fact, when I die, and if I go to heaven, I want the same dining arrangements.

Our lunch became an annual event, with sadly decreasing numbers. Even the indestructible Nugget is a bit frail. But he's not lost his zest for life nor his capacity to talk a leg off an iron pot when the mood takes him.

I just listen. Miller about Arthur Morris: 'I once bowled him eight bouncers in an over.

'There had been a lot of discussion in the press about short-pitched bowling. There was a lot of talk about banning it or limiting the number of bouncers so I thought I'd have a spot of fun.

'When Arthur came out to bat I put nine men on the square-leg boundary and came off my long run and just bowled at his head. When I bowled the first one Arthur said, "Oh dear, a bouncer." And every time I bowled another, he'd say, "Oh my God, he's done it again." And it so tickled me that I started laughing so much that the tears were running down my face as I came in to bowl. I could hardly make it to the crease. Old Arthur was in a right state.'

'Was Morris all right?' I enquired.

'All right?' said Miller. 'He hit me for 34 in the over.'

Fingo on opening for his club with the legendary Charlie Macartney: 'As he walked to the wicket, he said to me, "Now think on, young Fingleton, be ready first ball." I would have done anything for him but I wasn't

sure what he meant. Did he mean be prepared for a quick single? Was he telling me to concentrate from the first moment?

'All these questions were racing through my mind as the fast bowler raced in for the first ball and as he did I saw Macartney walking down the wicket with his bat at shoulder level.

'In an instant several things happened. The bowler bowled and Macartney, halfway down the wicket, gave it an awesome smack. The bowler dived for cover, so did I. The ball hit the sightscreen on the full and bounced back fifty yards on to the field of play.

'It was the most audacious shot I have ever seen. As I lay there alongside the fast bowler, who was by now a gibbering wreck, I looked up and saw the batsman standing above me tapping the wicket with his bat. "Just like I said, young Fingleton. Always ready from the first ball." He looked at the hapless bowler. "They don't like it you know," he said, confidentially.'

Lovely Jack. I did a couple of television shows with him in Australia and people demanded more. We persuaded him back for the third time but it worried him. He didn't think he could deliver again. Late at night, before the recording, he rang me. 'I don't know what to do that will be different.'

I tried to placate him. 'Jack, you'll think of something,' I said. He called back an hour later.

'I've been pondering what you said and I think I have the answer,' he said.

'What is it?' I asked.

'Ever had anyone croak on your show?' he asked.

What sums up Australia for me, and why I can't wait to get out there again, was a dinner I went to in an outback town during the last England tour.

I was asked to make a speech but as the time approached for me to sing for my supper it became apparent that proceedings were out of hand. The assembly was noisy and drunk and not about to be quiet to listen to another whingeing Pom.

The man introducing me tried hard to appeal for calm but with little effect. In desperation he tried his trump card. 'Come on guys, give the Pom a go,' he said. 'After all, it'll be better than a poke in the eye with a burnt stick.'

It was then I knew I had found my second home.

Jack Fingleton – sport at the highest level

THEY auctioned Jack Fingleton's baggy green the other day, the one he wore during the 1935–36 tour of South Africa when he scored three Test centuries. He made it four in a row – the first cricketer to do so – against England in the first Test of their 1936–37 tour of Australia.

Anyway, I bought the cap because Jack was an old and dear friend and because I always wanted to own a baggy green. It is the most famous cricket cap in the world, and the best looking.

There is no more defining and thrilling sight in cricket than the Aussies turning out in that distinctive head gear. It is both a trademark and a declaration that the men wearing it have earned it the hard way.

It will go nicely with the Aussie sweater Keith Miller gave me. He turned up for lunch once in Oz carrying a plastic bag. After the meal, as he stepped into a taxi home, he thrust the bag into my hands. 'I want you to have this, it doesn't fit me any more,' he said.

When I looked inside I was choked. I nearly burst into tears. I'm just an old-fashioned romantic, really, and the older I get the more reason I find to be so.

The cap arrived two days ago badly abused in transit. The plastic case it travelled in had been smashed and the peak of the cap was broken. I'm not sure if this was

caused by the journey or a Harold Larwood bouncer. Harold told me that Jack never flinched from the short stuff. In fact, what he said was, 'He was a tough little bugger. You couldn't knock him down.'

I worked with Jack on a Sunday newspaper in the sixties and early seventies, but really got to know him after he had retired. I was making a speech at the National Press Club in Canberra and invited questions. Pretending he didn't know me, Jack stood up and reduced the formality of the proceedings to a rubble.

His question (it lasted five minutes) included the observation that although I was a Pom I was at least a Yorkshire Pom, which wasn't so bad, although I came from Barnsley which, as everyone knew, had the highest illegitimacy rate on the planet and, what is more, was the birthplace of the groundsman who prepared the wicket at Headingley where Fred Trueman twice bowled out the Aussies to win a Test match which was clearly a fix, since the only way we could ever beat the Aussies was by cheating . . . and on, and on, and on.

All this was delivered out of the corner of the mouth and with twinkling eyes. He was a funny, cantankerous, wise and argumentative man. Like his great friend, Bill O'Reilly, he was afeared of no man, including Bradman.

He was a fine cricketer. In the first-class game he scored nearly 7,000 runs at 44. In Test cricket he averaged 42. He was also a marvellous observer of the game. Like Richie Benaud, he was a journalist by training and instinct – the best kind. In my list of favourite cricket writers he is among the top half dozen.

Watching Michael Vaughan bat at Lord's, I was reminded of an essay Jack wrote about Charlie Macartney. I am not about to compare Mr Vaughan with the man they called 'The Governor General'. We should be so lucky, and Michael Vaughan too. But there was something about Vaughan's posture against Ambrose and Walsh that declared his belief in himself as a Test-match cricketer. Sport at the highest level is as much a triumph of the will as a test of technique. Vaughan has it, perhaps Ramprakash doesn't.

Jack Fingleton said Macartney had it in abundance. As the next batsman went out to face a rampaging bowler, Macartney would tell him, 'Don't worry, I'll fix him.'

Macartney told Jack that every ball 'had a look on its face', as it came towards him. When Jack asked for an explanation, Macartney said, 'It was labelled either 1, 2, 3, 4, or 6. I leave out the 5. Too far to run.'

At the end of his career, he was told he had been one of the chosen few to appear in the Australian version of *Who's Who*. He replied, 'I have no desire to appear in any publication of this kind and I fail to see that any good purpose will be served by my name appearing.'

Jack's funny, revealing and perceptive essay on Macartney is published in a book he wrote called *Masters of Cricket*. Beg, borrow or steal as they say.

Fingleton's laconic manner made him a television natural. The first time I interviewed him he overdid the dental fixative required to stop his teeth clacking and spent an agonising hour in his hotel bathroom experi-

menting with various solvents so that he might unclamp his jaws. As he explained, it would have been embarrassing, to say the least, had he arrived on the set with appropriate fanfare only to say, 'G'Gay, Gichael.'

He died a year after his last appearance on my show. I miss him but not in a sad way. Whenever I think of Jack Fingleton I hear the echo of remembered laughter.

July 2000

Bill O'Reilly – the Tiger
keeps his claws sharpened

Bill O'Reilly recently had one of his legs amputated below the knee. It means, he tells me, that he will no longer be able to operate from his full run but otherwise he is bearing up.

He is in his eighties and neither cruel illness nor old age can change his feisty manner. He is a mettlesome man, full of opinion and argument. When I called to enquire about his condition he said, 'I just sit here watching the kitchen wall in case someone runs off with it. It is a very boring occupation but I have to tell you that it is infinitely more interesting than watching one-day cricket.'

For thirteen years, O'Reilly has been an implacable enemy of the pyjama game and an outspoken critic of the razzmatazz surrounding it. He treats any attempt to persuade him of the game's virtues with a contemptuous snort. And yet there is little doubt that in his pomp he would have been the perfect one-day bowler. He spun the ball from leg at little under medium pace, he made it bounce, he had perfect control and a fearsome competitive spirit, hence the nickname 'Tiger'.

After he retired from cricket he kept a critical eye open as a journalist and his opinions were what you might expect from a man who bowed to no one, including Don Bradman. Shortly after our conversation, a friend of mine persuaded him to be guest of honour at a

luncheon in the company of Ray Lindwall, Neil Harvey, Arthur Morris, Norman O'Neill, Rod Marsh, Alan Davidson, Mike Gatting, Godfrey Evans, Martin Donelly, Bill Brown, Alec Bedser and Ken Archer.

O'Reilly, in full flow, was asked about the modern curse of sledging opponents. 'Never spoke to an opponent on the field of play,' he said, 'except on one occasion when an English batsman called me a cheat.'

'Then what?' I enquired.

'It didn't happen again, that's what,' said O'Reilly, with an enigmatic smile.

Someone reminded him that in the sixties, when commenting on the Australia v. West Indies series, he supported Charlie Griffith when the fast bowler ran out Ian Redpath, who was backing up, without first warning him. He still thinks he was right, that any batsman seeking to take unfair advantage of a bowler deserves all he gets.

But he was reminded that during the Griffith row he was taken to task by his good friend, Jack Fingleton, who accused him of being provocative and asked what he would have done in a similar situation. The question was fanciful, said O'Reilly. 'How so?' enquired Fingleton. 'Because,' said Tiger with a twinkle, 'when I was bowling, the non-facing batsmen were never that eager to get down the other end.'

January 1991

Bill O'Reilly died on 6 October 1992 in Sydney.

Don Bradman – my
lifelong pursuit

THE other day I was talking to Jeff Thomson, the fast bowler, about Bradman, and Jeff said that in the 1970s he was at a social event organised by a man who owned a cricket field. During the afternoon, Sir Donald, then in his sixties, was approached by two young cricketers who were on the fringe of the state team. They asked Bradman if they could bowl at him. He pointed out he hadn't played for nearly thirty years, but eventually removed his jacket and picked up a bat.

At first, the young men bowled respectfully at him, aware both of his age and the fact he had neither pad nor gloves. But when Bradman started playing shots, they quickened up and eventually were bowling flat out. According to Thomson, the quicker they bowled, the harder Bradman smote them to the boundary.

Jeff said, 'It was bloody magnificent. All my life I had looked at his record and thought, "How can anyone be twice as good as Greg Chappell?" That day, I found out.'

March 1996

I have travelled long and far in my search for Donald Bradman. It started nearly fifty years ago when I rode

on my bike the thirty miles to Leeds to see his Australian team slaughter our lot.

Since the first glimpse I have been seeking an audience. I have telephoned, telegrammed (remember?), written, faxed, pleaded, ranted and cajoled. The answer has always been no.

I have offered money, attempted to lure him with limousines and expensive hotel suites, persuaded mutual friends to use their influence, even tried incense and prayer. I still haven't interviewed Sir Donald. Not even got close.

On the odd occasion when I have glimpsed him in the distance he vanished before I could reach him, like a mirage. Once or twice I have been somewhere only to be told he had just left. One time the host showed me the teacup he had been drinking from. The liquid was still warm. I felt like an explorer who had just found a fresh footprint of the Abominable Snowman.

Why so persistent? Because he was the greatest cricketer who ever lived and a significant man both in the history of the game and the development of his country. In cricket there have been two towering figures, two people who more than any other wrote the history of the game. They are W.G. Grace and D.G. Bradman. One is still with us and any journalist worth his salt has a duty to try to talk to him.

The other reason is much more selfish. In a lifetime of interviewing people I have talked to most of my heroes. The two big ones who escaped were Frank Sinatra

and Donald Bradman. I got closer to The Kid from Hoboken than I ever did to The Boy from Bowral.

But let us suppose that dreams come true and the interview has been arranged. What do I ask The Don? Well, all else apart, what fascinates me about Bradman is his fame. Generally speaking, being famous is a bit like having measles.

It is a minor affliction and the rash soon disappears. But for some it never goes away. It dictates their life and shapes their circumstances. They and their family are forever on display.

They are isolated by a special kind of celebrity and become icons of their time. Sir Donald Bradman belongs in that category.

I went looking for him on Australia Day in Adelaide. You must admire my stamina. Adelaide is his lair, the cricket ground on the first day of a Test match one of his regular watering-holes and therefore offering the best chance of a sighting.

A man I met said he would take me to have tea with Sir Donald in a box in the Bradman Stand. Overcome by emotion I clasped my new friend by the lapels and told him of my search for the Holy Grail.

A short time later he took me to one side and said he would have to ask Sir Donald if he minded having me in the box. I had obviously frightened him with my exuberance. He must have thought I was going to kidnap The Don or film him with a hidden camera picking his nose.

I told him not to bother Sir Donald with such petty

problems and settled instead for a drink in the Bradman Bar looking at pictures of the great man and wondering if they sold such a thing as a Bradman Burger.

Mooching around the ground I came upon my old friend Keith Miller making one of his rare public appearances.

He had just been to see Sir Donald. How was he? 'Looks fit enough to be still playing,' said Keith.

He invited me to his caravan parked on the tennis courts. Whenever there is a Test match at Adelaide Keith Miller sets up office in a caravan belonging to a friend and entertains the world.

Life is never dull in his company. People are attracted to him like iron filings to a magnet. His personality embraces everyone from bookmakers to conductors of great orchestras, barmaids to brain surgeons, people who sell newspapers on London streets and men who commanded armies in time of war.

If I was allowed to organise a party of people I most love and admire to celebrate my last day on earth, Keith Ross Miller would be at the top of the list.

His meeting with Sir Donald was a significant one. It might be the last time the two of them got together. Keith is in his mid-seventies, Sir Donald ten years older.

They played with and against each other and it was, at times, a fairly turbulent relationship; they were very different men. Miller was the maverick, Bradman the authoritarian.

Conflict was inevitable. In Sir Donald's last first-class game at Sydney, Miller greeted him with two bouncers.

The first, of the harmless variety, was hit for four. The second, preceded by a gesture to the press box declaring, 'If you think that was funny you ain't seen nothing yet,' nearly decapitated Sir Donald, who at the time happened to be chief selector.

The incident had nothing to do with the fact that Miller, then the world's greatest all-round cricketer, was not in the team to tour South Africa which was named a short time later.

Differences apart, what the two men have in common is a celebrity that travels far beyond the shoreline of Australia and represents much more than a reputation gained as flannelled fools.

What they symbolised in their prime, and still do today, is the Australian character at its very best. Bradman was the gifted Aussie battler, the man of few words but great deeds. Miller was the handsome, sun-kissed playboy who laughed at life and didn't give a stuff.

Bradman was the Outback and the fight against nature, Miller was Bondi Beach and a celebration of the good life.

There are a million funny anecdotes about Miller, not many about Don Bradman. The Bradman legend is built on stories underlining the prowess that set him apart from other men.

There is, for instance, the tale of Bill Black, an off-spin bowler playing for Lithgow who on a memorable day in 1931 bowled Bradman for 52. The umpire was so excited that when the ball hit Bradman's wicket he called out, 'Bill, you've got him.'

The ball was mounted and given to Bill Black as proof that he dismissed the greatest batsman in the world.

Later that season Don Bradman again played against Bill Black. As the bowler marked out his run, Don said to the wicket-keeper, 'What sort of bowler is this fellow?'

The wicket-keeper, a mischievous fellow like the rest of his tribe, replied, 'Don't you remember this bloke? He bowled you out a few weeks ago and has been boasting about it ever since.'

'Is that so?' said Bradman. Two overs later Bill Black pleaded with his skipper to be taken off. Bradman had hit him for 62 runs in two eight-ball overs. He made 100 in three overs and finished with 256 including 14 sixes and 29 fours.

The other side to his genius is demonstrated by an encounter with George Macaulay, the feisty Yorkshire seam bowler, in 1930. It was Bradman's first tour of England and there was a popular rumour that the English wickets would sort him out. As an ardent subscriber to this theory Macaulay couldn't wait to get at Bradman.

When Yorkshire played the Australians early in the tour Macaulay demanded loudly of his captain, 'Let me have a go at this bugger.' His first over was a maiden. Bradman then hit him for five fours in the second over and took 16 from the third. A spectator yelled, 'George, tha' should have kept thi' bloody trap shut.'

Macaulay was not the only English bowler to suffer on that tour. Harold Larwood once told me of a famous encounter with Bradman at Leeds during the third Test of the series when the little man played one of his great

innings. Harold said there was no doubt in his mind Bradman was the greatest batsman to whom he ever bowled.

'We worked on the theory he was uneasy against the short-pitched ball early on,' said Harold. 'Maurice [Tate] got Archie Jackson and they were two for one. I gave Bradman a short one first ball. He played at it and there was a nick. George Duckworth caught it. We thought we had him but the umpire didn't agree. Mind you, we got him out shortly after.'

'How many had he got?' I asked, walking blindfold into the trap.

'Three hundred and thirty-four,' replied Harold with a grin.

When I first wrote that story many years ago I received a letter from Sir Donald saying he was concerned I cast doubts on his sportsmanship. I had not intended to do so nor do I now. Indeed, Harold Larwood's telling of the story was done very much tongue-in-cheek and recounted to enhance the Bradman legend rather than diminish it. Nonetheless, Bradman's reaction was revealing.

It served as a reminder that for all his genius, or perhaps because of it, Bradman often seems a distant and remote hero, preferring to be admired rather than beloved. The statistical difference between him and other cricketers is not the only huge gap that exists betwixt Bradman and the game he adorned.

R.S. Whitington, who played under Bradman for South Australia and later became a writer and commentator on the game, once wrote: 'Bradman the man was

not so easy to idolise as Bradman the batsman. He decided . . . to remain encased in a shell that any oyster would have envied.'

To this day – and Bradman is now eighty-six years old – the greatest cricketer of all time has never given the long, definitive television interview about his life and time; a legacy to be stored in the national archives for future generations to watch and study.

He did a series of interviews about his career for radio, and fascinating they are too. But like the books written about his life, including his autobiography, they provide only a simple sketch of the man. Why should Bradman bother to go any deeper? Because he is not only an important figure in the history of cricket but a significant man in the development of his country.

No Australian has done more to announce his nation's pride and ambition. His effect on Australians during the Depression years alone is worthy of a book. A parody of the Lord's Prayer at the time went:

> Our Harbour which art in heaven
> Sydney be its name
> Our Bridge be done in 1930 or 1931
> Give Us this day our daily Bradman
> For ours is the harbour, the bridge and the Bradman for
>   ever and ever.

How close did I get to Sir Donald? Well, eventually I sat at one end of a box and he was fifteen people away.

I know. I counted. In profile he looked like a kooka-burra. It was interesting observing people's reaction to

his presence. Some sneaked photographs of him, while others blatantly turned their backs to the cricket and surveyed the great man.

I fell once more to contemplating the kind of fame attached to Sir Donald and began comparing it to Keith Miller's.

In the end it is the difference between being inspected and being celebrated. The trouble with national treasures is that they are often placed behind glass, isolated by protocol, protected by a self-appointed Papal Guard.

Sir Donald remains a remote and lonely figure whose life will be judged and assessed by archivists and historians for as long as the game of cricket is played. Keith Miller will be celebrated in song, joke and anecdote.

As I left the Adelaide Oval on Australia Day I was struck by the thought that any country capable of producing two such gifted and singular men has much to be proud of and great reason to celebrate.

January/February 1995

Sir Donald Bradman died on 25 February 2001 in Adelaide.

ALLAN BORDER – QUIET BUT RUTHLESS

For all his reputation as a stern captain and an implacable opponent, Allan Border is, like most Aussies, a friendly cove. The first thing you notice about him are his eyes, light and clear, giving a steely glint to an otherwise cherubic countenance. In the bar of the team hotel, his young players around him, there is no doubting his authority. A stranger breaks into a conversation Border is having, saying, 'Am I interrupting something?'

The players grin self-consciously at his unwitting rudeness. Border handles the intrusion with tact and diplomacy, making sure the visitor is not discomfited. I only mention these aspects of our meeting because if you had read the cuttings beforehand, as I did, this was not what you would expect. What you might have anticipated encountering was a surly individual with a liking for bollocking people who get in his way. In other words, Captain Grumpy.

Merv Hughes came into the bar, blocking out the light, a huge presence in what looked like a blue romper suit. His captain inspected him. 'Two stone overweight, funny haircut, ridiculous moustache, big oaf and do you know what? A captain's dream. He'd shed a pint of blood for you. I love him. He's my kind of cricketer. Good bowler too. People are only just beginning to realise what a fine bowler he is.

Allan Border

'Statistics show that of all Australian quick bowlers his strike rate is second only to Lillee. He makes my point about Test cricketers. They are forty per cent skill and sixty per cent character. You can have all the talent in the world and if you don't have the guts and determination to go with it you'll be nothing to me.

'I demand one hundred per cent from all my players all the time. I'm tough on anyone who is goofing off or not performing. I'm a fierce competitor, always have been, but it's not altogether about personal attitudes. We represent something important to the people of Australia. They want to be proud of us and we musn't fail them. "Only a game"? Don't give me that. After a Test match I go to the media conference and there's forty cameras there and fifty journalists, and you say it's only a game.

'It's a lot more important than just a sporting event to a lot of people. The difference between winning and losing nowadays is enormous. It might well have been that once upon a time you could be looked on as being gallant in defeat. Not now. You're rubbish if you lose. You cop it. Look at what's happening to Goochie at present.

'They call me Captain Cranky or Grumpy and worse, but it doesn't bother me. I suppose I've given them the reason to call me names from time to time. I've had the odd flare-up with umpires which I shouldn't have done. I knocked my stumps down at Lord's this year and that was silly. Once or twice I've lost my temper with journalists and called them pricks. Little things like that.

I've crossed the line a few times,' he said. What line might that be? 'Between being a hard-nosed competitor and a prat.'

For someone who professes to be shy of making speeches and who is happiest when surrounded by his players, he is an agreeable, pleasant and loquacious dinner companion. He has come a long way from being the gullible twelfth man for New South Wales who was persuaded that his duties involved interrupting play in order to take orders for the players' lunch.

He started his Test career against England by getting what he thought was a bad lbw decision. He stormed back to the pavilion, threw his bat across the room, kicked his pads into the corner and cursed the cheating Poms before realising that he was in the England dressing-room receiving some strange looks from the touring officials and players.

He took over as captain of Australia after Kim Hughes's tearful farewell. He had a tough baptism and nearly gave the job up in New Zealand on the 1985–86 tour. He says now that it took him a while to commit himself totally to the idea of being captain. New Zealand was 'a cry for help'. His salvation was winning the World Cup in 1987, followed by some serious soul-searching about what to do in England in 1989. He decided he needed to be much tougher. One of his decisions was to dissuade wives from travelling with their husbands.

'I took terrible flak for that. Towards the end of the tour some of the wives confronted me and told me what

they thought. I said, "At this time on the last tour of England we were 3–1 down. This time we're winning 3–0. End of story."' The rule still stands.

As he explains, he cannot stop wives travelling to where their husbands might be playing, but there is no question of them sharing the same hotel, or players attending to husbandly duties at the expense of team commitments. 'My wife is here now with the kids. She lives in Essex. Now and again she brings the kids to a game and we say "G'day" but that's it. The point is they're on holiday, we're working,' he said.

Border was even more tough with his players. While batting with Dean Jones in the tied Madras Test in 1986 when the Victorian scored a double century, he observed the player's distress. At one point Jones was so dehydrated he was throwing up.

'He had made about 180 at the time and I desperately wanted him to hang about a bit longer. He said he couldn't go on. So I said, "OK then, go off and send someone in with a big ticker." I knew that would anger him into staying because Jonesy prides himself on having a big heart. But I really didn't realise how crook he was.'

Jones stayed at the crease, completed his 200 and was taken from the field to hospital and put on a saline drip.

'I felt bad about it. I deliberately said what I did to goad him into staying but I really had no idea he was so ill. He's a tough competitor. He'd crawl over broken glass for you,' said Border. It says something for the strength of the Australian batting and the resolve of the selectors that Jones was not selected for this tour.

While on the subject of guts, I told Allan Border of Tom Graveney's assessment of him: 'A great player, particularly when it matters.' He liked that.

'Maybe being captain helped me with the batting. Maybe I was always aware of the added responsibility and that made me more determined to grit my teeth and play in a certain way. It would be lovely to play like David Gower, wouldn't it, or Mark Waugh? Make it look so easy, don't they?' They, no doubt, would wish to have scored as many as Border and equal his average of 51, which sets him apart as one of the great batsmen.

He may lack the grace and style of the likes of Gower and Waugh, he may not have the aura of a Richards or the personality of a Botham. What he is, *in excelsis*, is the good old Aussie battler. He's the tough little runt with the jutting chin and the unquenchable spirit. If you wanted a man to captain a team to play for your life, there would be only one choice.

'Captaining a side isn't all it's cracked up to be. Good captains are made by good teams. The best you can do is initiate a team structure, set a mood in the dressing-room. But you can be the most brilliant tactician and if you don't have a team you're bloody useless.

'I've enjoyed being captain. I never imagined I would be, so I was delighted when I got it. I like having the respect of the players. I suppose I shall have to start thinking soon about giving the game up. We play South Africa after the Ashes tour and I'd like to skipper the side. After that I might retire. I don't want to linger too long. On the other hand, I don't want to go too soon.

I know I won't like giving up the game. When I see these athletes who have just retired telling the media how happy they are I think they are talking absolute bullshit. You have to miss playing sport. It's such a wonderful life.

'I'd like to stay in the game. I don't want to be an administrator. I'm a player's person. I don't fancy the media. It seems to me that a lot of the old players who start commentating on the game become twice the players they really were. I'd feel uncomfortable with that. Meantime I don't have any goals. I'm a funny sort of person. I never set targets. Why set yourself 500 runs to get in a series? You might go out first knock and score 499. What do you do then? All my cricket ambitions centre around the team.'

What about the Ashes? 'I think we'll win. I'm not cocky enough or silly enough to predict the score but I do think we'll beat the Poms. I think we have the edge on bowling. McDermott and Hughes are as good an opening pair as you'll find. Our batters are in form. We're a happy team. We won the one-days, but you handed us two you should have won.

'England? Impressed by Caddick. Also liked the look of Salisbury. If England pick a keeper instead of Stewart I think Steven Rhodes is a good player. Got a big heart too. That's what you want. If I were picking the England team I'd pick some young players and perhaps be pre-pared to lose for a couple of seasons. Young players and Gatting. He'd be in my team.

'Whatever happens, this is special. I have never won

a Test series against the West Indies and that's an ambition, but there is clear daylight between that and competing for the Ashes. There's nothing like it, nothing more important, nothing with the same edge to it.'

The captain of Australia is relishing the battle ahead. Whenever he appears we should go out of our way to say farewell because we shall not see him as a player again, and if we see his like in the near future we will count ourselves lucky. I asked him if there was an athlete he admired.

'Björn Borg. I liked the contrast between his confidence on court and his shyness off it. I like to think I've got something of that character. Quiet, but ruthless.'

May 1993

Allan Border works for Fox Sport as a cricket commentator. He is a Board member of Queensland Cricket and an Australian selector. He represents Australia on the ICC cricket committee (playing).

MARK TAYLOR – JUST PLAYS CRICKET

WHEN the Australian cricket team arrived in England last year I was invited to introduce them at the welcoming press conference. Before we went on stage I was taken on one side and asked to try to shield Mark Taylor from the inevitable questions about his loss of form and lack of suitability for captaincy. I said in my experience Mark Taylor was more than capable of seeing off his critics without outside assistance and if by chance the Australians didn't want him he could come and play for us.

As it was he treated his tormentors with charm and intelligence, demonstrating, not for the first time, the difference in quality between himself and his critics. Mark Taylor is a class act and his recuperation in England was merely the overture to what he achieved in Pakistan.

When he arrived in Australia the other day it was to the passionate embrace of a grateful nation. That is putting it mildly. In a country where sporting success is everything, Mark Taylor has the keys to the kingdom. If the people voted for a president tomorrow he would be a shoo-in. The Prime Minister is his greatest fan, advertisers and sponsors are threatening to submerge him with money. Normally bilious phone-in hosts are honey at the mention of his name.

Good grief, he has even been mentioned in the same sentence as Sir Donald Bradman – the ultimate accolade. The funniest compliment (although Mark Taylor's management don't think so) was the advert for toilet paper appearing soon after he had scored his triple century which read: 'Tubby, It's Good To See You In The Runs Again!'

An advertising man said Taylor could now make as much as he liked selling whatever he wanted because he had the perfect image: quality, reliability and triumph over adversity.

None of it is likely to change Mark Taylor. No sportsman of my acquaintance has more clearly demonstrated an ability to treat failure and success in the same levelheaded way. Others may talk of them being imposters, Mark Taylor is familiar with both and holds the two of them by the throat at arm's length.

It was only eighteen months ago at Heathrow airport when an immigration officer said to Mark Taylor, 'Ah, Mr Taylor, the captain.' 'That's right,' said Mark. 'But for how long?' came the reply.

It was a question he faced when he went out to bat against Derbyshire before the first Test match. He was out of form and seriously contemplating not only giving up the captaincy but retiring from international cricket. He nicked a wide half-volley from Phil DeFreitas and Dean Jones dropped him at first slip. Taylor walked down the wicket and said to Justin Langer. 'That's it. I'm ready to give up.'

Langer told him to stop talking rubbish and start

battling, which is what he did. He made 63, scored a century in the first Test and took his team to victory in the series. Had Jones caught the ball it might have been a very different story for Mark Taylor. And he knows it, which is why he keeps an open countenance in both triumph and adversity.

If one gesture in Pakistan summed up the man, it was declaring the Australian innings closed with his score on 334. One more run and he had beaten the mighty Bradman. One more run and never mind fame, he was immortal. He will be forever remembered for the record he didn't break. Was it a gracious gesture, an acknowledgement of the unique status of Australia's most famous sportsman? Or was it Mark Taylor doing what he has always done, making a decision based on giving his team the best chance of winning? We'll never know, but there's a book or two, not to mention a mini-series, in the speculation.

In the final analysis the record will show that Taylor was one of the greatest of all Australian captains, one of the most prolific run-scorers and a man with few equals at first slip.

In many ways those are the least of his achievements. In my view his most profound and important contribution has been to demonstrate that good sportsmanship and success are not incompatible, that good guys do come first, that it is possible to withstand the so-called 'pressures' of modern sport without becoming a pain in the backside.

What Mark Taylor represents can only be accommo-

dated by old fashioned words like decency, honour, modesty, chivalry even. He is not a soft touch. You don't get to captain Australia unless you can fight. But what he has never done is lose sight of the fact that he is playing a game. Playing it for a living might be different from doing it for love, but not so you have to sell your soul to succeed.

While Mark Taylor was setting an example in Pakistan, John McEnroe was behaving like a prat in Australia. Playing in some gimmicky tennis tournament for fading stars, he revealed that he had lost none of his ability to abuse officials. His foul language and confrontational demeanour were suitable reminders of what can happen to a game when it is abused by its participants. His molly-coddling by the media was yet another indication of how villains are transformed into heroes. If you want the doomsday scenario of this trend, then just look at what is happening in English football.

McEnroe and those who seek to emulate his behaviour (and those who celebrate it) are the graffiti artists of sport. They leave it the uglier for their presence.

Mark Taylor stands apart from such skulduggery. If this makes him appear a quaint, isolated figure among modern sporting heroes then that is the biggest compliment he can be paid. He is a reminder of virtues we have either forgotten or reject for fear of appearing unfashionable.

Brisbane and the first game against England will be Mark Taylor's one hundredth Test match. It might be

his last series. What he has earned is the right to retire in his own time and of his own choosing.

Mark Taylor's young son was once asked at school what his father did for a living. 'Not much,' he replied, 'he just plays cricket.' Like father, like son. I'll bet when Dad does finally retire he will regard his son's assessment as the perfect epitaph.

November 1998

Mark Taylor made the change from player to commentator on Channel 9 alongside Richie Benaud. He is on the Board of Cricket, New South Wales and is a successful businessman.

Shane Warne – Australia's jewel in the crown

In the television lights Shane Warne glistened like a precious stone. The grey-green eyes sparkled, the diamond in his left ear twinkled and the gold chain round his neck glowed. He looked like he belonged in the vault of a bank rather than the over-crowded and stifling room of the after-match press conference.

His skipper Mark Taylor said, 'He is a bit of a wizard.' Mr Taylor was asked if he was pleased Shane Warne was in his team. I was sitting next to the captain of England who said *sotto voce*, as if in prayer, 'I wish he was in my bloody side.'

Shane Warne was asked about pressure. He looked bemused, as well he might. The only pressure he is under right now is to stay alive long enough to take more wickets than any other player who ever spun a cricket ball.

There is an appealing, mischievous quality about Warne. He spins a tale like he does a ball. He would have us believe he has invented a new kind of delivery, and when asked if it had been used to dismiss any English batsmen, smiled enigmatically and said it might have accounted for a couple.

He is not the first spin bowler to float propaganda as

Shane Warne

a means of causing confusion. After all, misdirection is at the heart of all magic and Warne is nothing if not a magician. John Gleeson, another Australian spin bowler of a different era, also invented a mystery ball, or so he alleged. Upon his retirement he was asked to come clean. 'Whatever it was, I couldn't make the ball turn into a pigeon.' Even at close of play he wasn't letting on.

I once asked Wilfred Rhodes how much he spun the ball. 'Enough,' he said. I pressed on. 'What was enough?' He said, 'If the batsman *thought* it was turning, that was enough.'

During the match I sat next to Bill Brown, a sprightly eighty-four year old, who captained Australia and opened the innings in the Bradman era. He thought Clarrie Grimmett was still the finest leg-spin bowler of them all but that Shane Warne was learning fast.

He said Grimmett had more variation and subtlety of flight, tempting victims like a fisherman casting for trout. If Grimmett lured, then Warne goes hunting with a net and broadsword, cornering his opponents with ceaseless hostility and resolve, forever probing nerve and sinew. How else to excuse the shot played by Graham Gooch who, for all his experience, finally became exasperated with Warne's unremitting persistence?

I asked Geoffrey Boycott how he might have played Warne. 'My tactic would have been to have taken a single as soon as possible and observe him from the other end,' he said.

November 1994

Australians are now the kings of cricket and their jewel in the crown is Shane Warne. I cannot remember a time when I enjoyed watching anyone explore the art and craft of spin bowling more than I did Warne this season. It seems to me he is now at the very peak of his talent, certainly the greatest spin bowler I have ever seen.

He goes about his business with an action as plain and functional as his bowling is complex and imaginative. In other words, the approach to the wicket gives nothing away, unlike Bishen Bedi's glide-in which announced a mastermind at work or Mushtaq Ahmed's bouncy, wristy signature. Warne's greatest gift and that which sets him apart from all other bowlers of his kind is his ability to attack the batsman constantly while bowling tight. No matter what the state of the game or the wicket, he is always at the batsman's throat.

His partnership with Ian Healy is one of the wonders, the great joys, of the modern game. Purists might like a little less chat between the two but no one can deny the almost telepathic understanding between them; the manner in which one is constantly posing new riddles and the other instantly solving them.

August 1997

Shane Warne had taken over 450 wickets for Australia by June 2002 and was chosen as one of *Wisden*'s five cricketers of the twentieth century.

TOUCHED BY
THE GODS

KEITH MILLER – THE
ULTIMATE HERO

FATHER time has no heroes. If he had then Keith Miller wouldn't now be so bad on his pins. He uses a frame to perambulate around his house and a stick when he takes the odd walk. In recent years he has fought cancer, arthritis and a stroke. 'Bloody wreck really,' he says. Not him. There is strength in the handshake, laughter in the voice, and the tilt of the chin and the challenge in the blue eyes belong to a man who has reached seventy-five without ever taking a backward step. I first saw him in 1945 with the Australian Services team. He was tall, long-legged, broad-shouldered and incredibly handsome. When he batted he hit the ball with great power and classical style. He bowled like the wind and caught swallows in the field.

I was smitten. He was my hero. Fifty years on and nothing has changed. I still think he was the most glorious cricketer I ever saw. John Arlott summed it up when he said, 'If I had my choice of a player to win a match off the last ball, whether it required a catch, a six or a wicket, I would pick only one player: Keith Ross Miller.'

When I called him to arrange the visit, England had just lost in Brisbane. Shane Warne was the new hero of Australian cricket. 'We will talk about Mr Warne,' he said on the phone. When I arrived at his mellow and quiet house above Newport Beach in Nullaburra Road

Keith Miller

on Sydney's North Shore, he led me to his study which contains the only memorabilia he considers worthy of display. There is a photograph of the Australian Services team taking the field at Bramall Lane, Sheffield, just after the war – Miller, Hassett, Pepper, Carmody and Sismey, all young and smiling in the Yorkshire sunlight. Underneath is pinned the cover of a magazine showing the war hero Guy Gibson, VC, DSO, DFC, sitting in a field of red poppies.

Keith Miller was deeply affected by the Second World War. It changed him. It gave him an insight into human nature and a set of values that have lasted until the present time. The way he played his cricket in the immediate post-war years was as much a celebration of surviving the war as it was the product of an impulsive nature and a lifelong desire never to be bored either by a person or a game. Keith Miller embraced life passionately because he had seen the alternative.

As much as he loved cricket, he never believed it was anything more than a game. This philosophy made him the darling of the fans but also brought him into conflict with those for whom cricket was more a business than a pleasure.

Donald Bradman was one such. Miller remembers that his first Test match was at Brisbane against Hammond's side. Australia made a massive score and then it rained and, in those days of uncovered pitches, England were caught on a sticky wicket. Miller said, 'It was unplayable. I took seven wickets but Blind Joe could have taken ten. My old mate Bill Edrich was playing.

He had a serious war and he survived and I thought, "He's my old Services mate. The last thing he wants after five years in the war is to be flattened by a cricket ball," so I eased up. Bradman came up to me and said, "Don't slow down, Keith. Bowl quicker." Do you know, that remark put me off Test cricket? Never felt the same way about it after that.'

He didn't do badly for someone not very interested in playing Tests. His record shows that in 55 matches he scored 2,958 runs at an average of about 37, and 170 wickets at 22.97. Like so many others, the war robbed him of his ripening years and there is no knowing what he might have achieved. On the other hand, to judge Miller, the cricketer, by looking at statistics is a bit like judging a writer by the number of books he has written. It misses the point. When the Centenary Tests between Australia and England took place, an English newspaper conducted a poll asking people to nominate the cricketers they would most like to see in their dream team. Keith Miller came top by a long way. Bradman was second.

If there is anyone in modern cricket with Miller's star quality and commercial potential it is Shane Warne. They represent vastly different eras – Miller the Brylcreem Boy, Warne the Nike Kid – but they share a glamour and a talent to entertain which are both rare and priceless. Keith Miller was keen to talk about Warne. He had made little notes on yellow paper so he wouldn't forget what he had to tell me.

First up, he thought that Warne was the biggest spin-

ner of a cricket ball he had ever seen, a great bowler. On the other hand, he thought the Poms played him with too much reverence. He said, 'I was over in England last year having my portrait painted for Lord's and I was guest of honour at a dinner. I told them then that they had better start sending their batsmen to the Fred Astaire School of Dancing if they wanted to play Shane Warne. In other words, use their bloody feet. You could see what I meant at Brisbane. The Englishmen played him from the crease. He dominated them and will continue to do so unless they attack him.

'When I first saw Warne bowl he took one for 160 against the West Indies. But I was impressed by his accuracy and the fact that he tried to spin the ball. I called Tiger O'Reilly and asked him what he thought. He agreed. Tiger had been praying for years for a great spin bowler to emerge. I imagine that today he is looking down on us and saying "halleluja".'

Miller said it was absurd for any side to become as dominated by a bowler as England appeared to be by Warne. He would love to see the present Australian batsmen, the likes of Slater and Mark Waugh, playing Warne. 'We have the best crop of young batsmen in Australia I can ever remember. In my time there were Bradman, McCabe, Archie Jackson. At present we have about ten young players of enormous talent. They are quick-footed, aggressive, a delight to watch.'

Miller said that when Allan Border retired he would have appointed Dean Jones as the next Australian captain. He thought it a pity that Jones's career had been

cut short because of his inability to bite his tongue. He no doubt sees parallels in his own life. In the opinion of many good judges, Richie Benaud included, Miller was the best captain Australia never had, but the playboy who delighted the audience terrified the establishment. After all, this is the captain of the New South Wales team who led his men on to the field and ordered them to scatter. He smiles at the memory. 'Perfectly true, but you have to remember that my team knew their places in the field,' he said. All right then, but what about the time twelve came on to the field and when told of his mistake Miller said, 'One of you bugger off, the rest scatter.' Alan Davidson, the great Australian all-rounder who played in that game, recalls that when Miller arrived in the middle after issuing his famous instruction he turned around to find he was the only player on the field.

Then there was the occasion when Miller got so drunk the night before the big game, celebrating the birth of a son, that he arrived late at the ground, ran on the field with a colossal hangover with his bootlaces slapping and took 7 for 12 to win the match. And what about that day in England when he was asked to present the cup at the Greyhound Derby and arrived at the track from a wedding wearing morning coat and top hat? He backed the winner and made his way to the podium where he picked up the successful dog and kissed it on the nose.

There are a thousand stories like that making up the legend of Keith Miller, but I'll tell you just two more to sum him up and illustrate precisely why he never captained his country. At Manchester, on the tour domi-

nated by Jim Laker, Australia faced a deficit of 375 runs in the first innings. With Laker rampant it was a lost cause. Ian Johnson, the Australian captain, tried a pep talk. He told his team, 'We can fight back. We need guts and determination. We can still save this match.' Keith Miller was studying a racing guide at the time. He looked up. 'Bet you 6–4 we can't,' he said.

On Bradman's tour in 1948, Australia made 721 runs in a day against Essex. All the Aussies filled their boots except Miller, who walked to the wicket, didn't take guard, lifted his bat and let the ball hit the stumps. He said to the wicket-keeper, 'Thank God that's over,' and walked off. Raiding sweetshops wasn't his style. A noble sentiment, but it cost him dear.

Nonetheless it has been a 'helluva good life' he says. He has been married for forty-eight years to Peg, his intelligent and charming American wife. They live within reach of their sons, seven grandchildren and one great-grandchild. Speaking personally, I would have ennobled him long ago for his services to cricket, his dedicated support of the brewing and bloodstock industries, and his significant contribution to the gaiety of life. He is delighted with the portrait commissioned by the MCC, not so much by the likeness – 'I look an old bugger' – but by the fact that it hangs in the Long Room over the entrance to the bar. A copy is furled in a tube in the corner of his study. I doubt if it will make it on to the wall with Bramall Lane and Guy Gibson.

He starts ticking off the faces on the Bramall Lane photograph. Most of them are dead. He points to Graham

Williams, a spindly figure. 'Tall fella, no flesh on him because he'd just been released from a prisoner-of-war camp where he'd been for four years. He'd only been back two weeks and here he was playing cricket at Lord's. When he walked out to bat the whole ground rose to him and applauded him all the way to the middle. It was the most touching moment of my life. I often wonder what must have been going through Graham's mind. Here he was, being cheered all the way to the middle, playing cricket at Lord's when he must have been thinking, "Am I really alive? Is this really happening? Am I dreaming?" I think of it often and it always brings tears to my eyes.'

There are two more photographs in the room. They show Miller and another pilot standing in front of the Mosquito and Beaufighter aircraft they flew during the war. He keeps them to remind him that he was one of the lucky ones who made it back. I asked him if it was true that after one raid over Germany he flew his Mosquito in a detour over the town where Beethoven was born in an act of homage to his favourite composer. 'Perfectly true and why not?' he said, which is probably what he said when reprimanded by his commanding officer back in England.

Miller's love affair with England has deepened over the years. He says he only met one Englishman he didn't like. It will be difficult to think of even one Englishman who didn't like Keith Miller. Of all the Australians to visit our shores he is the best loved, the most welcome. On the morning of his birthday he was on the phone for nearly four hours, many of the calls coming from

England. There are many reasons for his popularity, not least his outlook on life, summed up by a favourite saying: remember only the happy hours.

While we are looking at the picture taken at Sheffield all those years ago and he is naming the players for me, he comes to his own image and says, 'That's a bloke called Miller. I wish to God I looked like that now.' In the picture Miller is carefree and laughing, every inch of him proclaiming a formidable athlete.

I wanted to tell him that when people thought of him that was what they remembered, that no one who ever saw him play the game of cricket would forget the image of Miller in his pomp. But I didn't, lest he damn me as a silly old sod; or, more likely, regarded me quizzically and said, 'Lay you 6–4 they don't.'

December 1994

Keith Miller lives in New South Wales, but still makes occasional trips to England.

DENIS COMPTON – A
SPORTING GENIUS

To Lord's. Always a thrill but for the first time in a new season, a moment to treasure. The stateliest and loveliest of grounds. The occasion was the annual dinner of the Middlesex County Cricket Club presided over by Denis Compton. In truth, he was the reason I was there.

My love of the county started with him way back in the forties when he was the Biggles of English cricket. Every day when the sun shone he scored a century, and when he didn't his team-mate, Bill Edrich, did.

His face advertising Brylcreem beamed down from every hoarding. In those drab, post-war years he gave us what we had been starved of, excitement and glamour.

We were wary of him in Yorkshire. My old man reckoned he was a bit too flash. There was also a general feeling in the county that lusty cricketers were unsuited for the advertising of a gentleman's hair cream when it was well known that the best cure for unruly hair was a coating of Vaseline or a dab of axle grease.

But the main reason why Yorkshire displayed a grudging admiration for Denis was that he took some of the limelight from Len Hutton. The debate about who was the best player seemed to me to be futile.

It was like running a competition to find out if Beethoven was a finer composer than Mozart or Stanley

Matthews a better winger than Tom Finney. Nonetheless, whenever Denis appeared in Yorkshire there was the feeling that the young pretender had come to claim his title.

I remember one marvellous day at Bramall Lane in the days when we parked our bums on the terracing of the soccer stand and were united, not only in discomfort, but by a common desire for Len to score a hundred and Denis to get out early on.

As it was, with Middlesex fielding, a dog ran on the field and stopped play. It was a Sheffield mongrel, a hound of very dubious parentage, and it headed towards Denis as if it knew him. Denis swooped, picked the dog up and, holding it aloft, ran towards the pavilion.

In those days Denis caught everything, including stray dogs. He was making his triumphant journey when the dog squirmed in his grasp and gave him a nasty bite in the arm.

The Bramall Lane crowd had observed everything in disapproving silence until the mongrel turned on Denis, whereupon one member of the Len Hutton Appreciation Society bellowed across the field, 'Put some bloody Brylcreem on it, Denis.'

Later on I saw him batting, sometimes improvising like a jazz musician and every so often leaning into a cover drive of classic style just to remind us that, as with all great players, the foundation of his genius was a marvellous technique.

April 1993

I T was clearly season's end at Lord's. The staff were busy wrapping up the ground for winter and even though the sun shone there was a nip in the air. A few spectators sat quietly as Middlesex and Gloucestershire performed the closing ritual to another season.

On a balcony, high in the Mound Stand, sat an old man with white hair and carrying a stick. Drink in hand, he looked down on the scene. At the age of seventy-six, Denis Compton was surveying his kingdom. In his pomp he did not simply play at Lord's, he possessed it. When he walked to the middle he was not a cricketer coming out to bat on his home turf, he was an impresario performing a one-man show in an auditorium he owned.

There are bits of Denis Compton all over Lord's, reminders – if ever we needed them – of his glory days. There is, most spectacularly, the stand bearing his name at the Nursery End.

In the MCC archive there is an old biscuit tin containing the knee cap that Denis Compton had removed in 1955. I was unaware this treasure existed and so, I suspect, are the majority of cricket lovers. It prompted the thought, however, that when they start preserving bits a player has had surgically removed and storing them in vaults like saints' bones, then we are clearly talking about someone of unusual significance.

Nearly forty years ago Compton's knee was big news, a matter for national concern. So much so that the orthopaedic surgeon who performed the operation, Osmond Clarke, kept Compton's patella as a souvenir and would show it to visitors to his consulting rooms. Before he

died, Clarke sent the knee cap to Gubby Allen, who placed it in the MCC archive. There it resides to this day in its tin bearing the legend 'Contents – One Knee Cap'.

When you mention his knee cap, Denis Compton shakes his head and smiles ruefully. He remembers that the problem started in 1938 when he collided with the Charlton goalkeeper, one Sid Hobbins. Many years later, when Compton's knee was newsworthy, Hobbins wrote to Compton. 'Dear Mr Compton, I am terribly sorry for the trouble I have caused you over the years. I am very sorry indeed. Sincerely, Sid Hobbins.'

'It wasn't his fault,' says Compton. 'But it obviously nagged him all those years.' In fact there can be little mystery to Hobbins's remorse. What happened was that in 1938 he collided with a fellow pro. But at the end of the 1940s, after Compton's golden summer of '47, he was aware he had lamed a hero.

Compton's reputation is, of course, founded on a much broader base than his achievements in one season, yet there is little doubt that the very special place he occupies in the mythology of the game has to do with the glamour and excitement he brought to the dreary and plain immediate post-war years.

Neville Cardus wrote: 'Never have I been so deeply touched on a cricket ground as I was in this heavenly summer when I went to Lord's to see a pale-faced crowd, existing on rations, the rocket bomb still in the ears of most folk – see this worn, dowdy crowd watching Compton. The strain of long years of anxiety and

affliction passed from all hearts at the sight of Compton in full sail . . . There were no rations in an innings by Compton.'

Compton remembers Cardus with affection. 'He used to seek me out. He would say to me, "You make me feel young."' It was a prescient remark. Even today, white hair, limp, stick and all, Compton has a mischievous, almost raffish air. He is one of those people who, when he arrives somewhere, never seems likely to stay very long.

Sometimes he doesn't arrive at all. He once turned up for lunch at a cricket match at close of play. 'Sorry I'm a trifle late old boy,' he explained to the host.

He said the same thing when he arrived for net practice at Old Trafford as the England team were finishing dinner. Compton had been instructed to turn up for practice in Manchester at 3 p.m. An hour before the appointed time he was in Sussex on holiday with his children. He persuaded a friend, who owned a light aircraft, to fly him to Manchester. The plane set off but had to make an emergency landing at Derby and he eventually arrived in time for coffee and liqueurs at the eve-of-Test dinner.

Peter May, his skipper, was not amused. What Compton dared not tell him or Gubby Allen, the chairman of selectors, was that he didn't have any kit. The plane was a small one and he had been forced to leave his cricket bag at the airport. The next day he borrowed a bat from Fred Titmus and scored 158 against the South Africans. In the second innings he made 71.

It was this daredevil quality about Compton that made him attractive and irresistible. In a film about his younger days he would have been played by someone as dangerous and dashing as Errol Flynn. The Compton we saw at Lord's the other day, full of mellow charm and gentle twinkle, would need to be played by Maurice Chevalier at his most agreeable.

The majority of those who turned up at Lord's for a party held in his honour had seen him play, but there were some, brought by their fathers or attracted by the legend, who were born long after he had retired. I observed one or two of them watching him, wondering no doubt what it was about this old man that made him such a significant hero. I wanted to help them but it would have taken too long, involving an explanation of long-forgotten days when men of exceptional talent could play for their country at both cricket and soccer – and all that the rest of us needed to be as successful and sexy was a dab of Brylcreem.

Compton wasn't quite the last of the double internationals but he was the greatest. There is no more compelling image of the all-round athlete *in excelsis* than Compton returning from the South African tour of 1948–49, having scored a triple-century and averaging 84.80 for the series, and stepping into the Arsenal team that won the Cup in 1950.

He doesn't care much for soccer nowadays. The romance has gone. He liked watching George Best but that was a while ago. In cricket he admires the energy and aggression of young Darren Gough and thinks that

Shane Warne might rank alongside O'Reilly. He can think of no higher praise. He would have left Graham Gooch out of the team to tour Australia but would have included Neil Fairbrother.

'I saw him make a most marvellous century and I said to Ted Dexter, who was then the chairman of selectors, that we had just seen the player who would bat at number five for England for many years to come. And Dexter said, "Oh no, I don't agree, I think Fairbrother is simply a one-day player." I couldn't believe it,' he recalls, shaking his head.

I wonder if nowadays the same judgement might not be made about Denis Compton. In these times of theory and analysis, when coaches are gurus and the commentators become oracles of the game, what judgement would they pass on a man who delighted in sweeping the ball off his middle stump, could not resist hooking the bouncer, and who once fell over in the middle of a shot and while flat on his back late-cut the ball, one-handed, for four? Might they not come to the conclusion that he lacked the application to be a Test match cricketer and that he was ideally suited to carnival cricket?

But back to Compton at Lord's the other day. It was good to see him, drinking champagne, surrounded by admirers, enjoying himself. He rolled back the years. That is his knack. There is a lovely story in the book about Denis receiving his CBE from The Queen after his retirement from the game. 'Oh, Mr Compton, how is your poor head?' she said. Denis thought for a

moment she was enquiring about his hangover and wondered how she came by the information.

Then he realised she was talking about an incident that had happened more than ten years earlier when, in 1948, he was struck on the head by a ball from Ray Lindwall. The point of the anecdote is that the genius of real heroes is to convince all of us, even monarchs, that it was only yesterday we saw them play.

September 1994

Denis Compton died on 23 April 1997.

GARFIELD SOBERS – SIMPLY THE BEST

THE last time I was in Barbados Michael Holding bowled that over to Geoffrey Boycott [1980–81 – five unplayable balls followed by a sixth that took Boycott's off stump]. So it's been a while. In the meantime they have built a wonderful new golf course on the site of an old sugar plantation. Robert Trent Jones Jr, the designer, says the Royal Westmoreland is one of his best and, without claiming an intimate knowledge of all he has done, I would find it difficult to imagine anything more beautiful or testing.

Mr Trent Jones had the good sense to name one hole after Sir Garfield Sobers. A plaque on the seventh says the Garfield Sobers hole is 365 yards long to celebrate the player's best Test score, made against Pakistan, which stood as the highest in Test cricket until Brian Lara came along. Sir Garfield regularly makes four here. In fact, he regularly makes par and better on most of the holes at the Royal Westmoreland. He is a formidable opponent off a handicap of nine plus a game leg and a bad eye.

It was good to see him again. He was the greatest cricketer there has ever been. There has been no other in the history of the game to match his all-round talent and versatility. In every other sport there is unending debate about the best. In soccer, was Pele better than Maradona, Finney the equal of Best? In boxing, would

Ali have beaten Marciano, could Tyson hold a candle to Joe Louis? Was Rod Laver a better tennis player than Björn Borg, and who was the best golfer there has ever been? Nicklaus, Palmer, Bobby Jones? Such was the talent of Garry Sobers that ever since he started playing the game the only question was who came second on the list.

It is difficult to explain to anyone who didn't see him play just how good he was. They immediately suspect you of exaggeration. The fact is he could have been selected as a Test cricketer in any of three categories: batsman, opening bowler and left-arm spinner capable of bowling in two different styles. He was also a magnificent fielder, particularly close to the wicket, where he stood comparison with the best of all time. Had he tried his hand at wicket-keeping we might never have heard of Alan Knott.

When we yarned the other day, I recalled the time I played alongside him in a charity game at Edgbaston. On a perfect summer's day in front of a large crowd our team chased over every inch of Warwickshire as the home county made more than 350. My only moment of glory came when I bowled Alvin Kallicharran. When he came to the wicket Garfield, who was standing at slip, shouted, 'Bowl him the bouncer Parky, he doesn't like it early on.' He was, of course, joking. I took him seriously and, in attempting to put one round Kallicharran's ears, bounced the ball in my half of the pitch, whereupon it floated towards the batsman who made two full swings before it bounced for a second time with

just enough forward impetus to fall against the middle stump. Later Kallicharran was gracious enough to say he had never seen anything like my delivery in a long and distinguished first-class career.

So it was with light heart and a spring in my step I went to open our innings in front of a crowd of 10,015 people, which was 10,000 more than I had played in front of before. Opening the bowling for Warwickshire was Bob Willis, who had just come back to the game after an injury. Given his lay-off and the convention of professional cricketers, particularly fast bowlers, not doing anything silly when playing against amateurs, I took guard and awaited the gentle half-volley for the courtesy one off the mark.

The ball did hit the bat but I didn't see it. I looked hopefully down the wicket at Willis for some indication he was having a bit of fun. He gave me a snarl. The next ball was equally fast and straight and knocked my wicket down.

I was sitting in the pavilion composing a poison pen letter to Mr Willis when Garfield Sobers sat next to me. He was padded up and ready for battle. 'Do me a favour?' I asked.

'What's that?' he said.

'Give Willis some stick,' I said.

When he went out to bat, Willis returned to the attack. Shortly after he bowled his first ball to Sobers, the world's greatest cricketer had made 50. Not much after that he had made 100. One shot against Willis remains in the memory. It wasn't a bad ball – on a

length, off and middle – but Sobers hit it with a long, flowing swing of the bat. It went past Bob's nose as he followed through and hit the sightscreen on the full before he had time even to look startled.

Lord's 1973, England versus West Indies, and I had seen him do much the same thing to Willis, as well as Geoff Arnold, Tony Greig, Derek Underwood and Raymond Illingworth. He scored 150 in what was his last great Test innings in England. That was the game when the crowd joined Dickie Bird in guarding the pitch during a bomb scare.

In the last session on Saturday, Sobers put Kallicharran on the boundary and ordered Keith Boyce to bounce Boycott. In those days Geoff liked to hook. He took the challenge and was caught on the boundary.

It would be fair to say that Boycott's actions did not please his skipper, Illingworth. The next day was Sunday and I had invited Illingworth and Boycott to lunch. Raymond arrived at the appointed time. He said, 'I don't think Geoff will be coming.' He explained that after a frank exchange of views at close of play he doubted if the England batsman was talking to him. We waited an hour or so and then decided to eat. It should be understood that Mr Illingworth has a remarkable appetite. He can trough more beef than Desperate Dan. I had just carved him the last portion when Boycott appeared at the door. 'Christ,' said Illingworth. 'I'm going to be popular. I've not only given him the bollocking of a lifetime, I've just eaten his bloody lunch.'

Garfield Sobers is eager for Yorkshire gossip. He was

the first overseas player ever to wear the white rose. It happened in the seventies when Yorkshire went on a tour of the Caribbean and persuaded him out of retirement to play for them. He has a great liking and admiration for Boycott, thinks Fred Trueman was as good a bowler as he ever faced and laughs fondly at the memory of Close.

'A great competitor. Mentally very tough. I liked playing against him,' said Garfield. Their most remarkable encounter occurred during the 1966 West Indies tour of England when the Yorkshireman replaced Colin Cowdrey as England captain for the final Test, with England three down. When Sobers came out to bat, Close gave the ball to John Snow and said, 'Bounce him Snowy. This fella can't hook.'

It should be explained that at the moment Sobers took guard he had scored 722 runs in the series at an average of 103. Moreover, he had taken 20 wickets at 27.25 and made 10 catches. Close's exhortation was so outrageous that thirty years on Garfield still can't work out whether he was blinded by tears of laughter or rage. In any event, he mis-hooked Snow's first ball straight into the hands of Close. It was one of the few times that Garfield Sobers allowed us to imagine he might be mortal after all.

Like all great athletes, he was a lord of time and space. In other words, he played in an environment of his own choosing at a rhythm dictated by his own mood and inclination. He was beautiful to watch no matter what he was doing on the field of play. He was blessed

with the natural, unhurried ease of movement that, along with an absence of frill or flourish, is the hallmark of the true stylist. He was everything an athlete should be: graceful and gracious, outrageously talented and naturally modest. Perhaps his most attractive and endearing attribute was he didn't understand what all the fuss was about. Still doesn't.

Yet for twenty years he played in every climate on all kinds of wickets against the best players in the world to establish himself as the undisputed champion of cricket.

If he has a weakness it is a fondness for the company of bookmakers and the advice of jockeys. He doesn't much like talking about cricket but becomes animated when discussing Lester Piggott, who he believes was the greatest jockey that ever drew breath.

He seems to exist on the periphery of West Indian cricket – and that is probably a generous assessment – which is sad when you consider his place in the history of the game. Apart from improving his handicap, his only recurring problem nowadays is dealing with people who claim a kinship to Malcolm Nash, the unfortunate Glamorgan bowler whom Sobers hit for six sixes in one over during a county match at Swansea.

While we were nattering in the clubhouse at the Royal Westmoreland, a man approached claiming to be Malcolm's cousin and asking to shake the great man's hand. 'Wherever I go I meet Malcolm's relatives. Must be a huge tribe,' said Garfield.

He is, of course, revered in Barbados: the unofficial king of the island. When he drove me to my hotel the

porters and security men were falling over themselves to be near him. After he had gone and the staff had quietened down, an American tourist who had witnessed the palaver approached me and asked what was going on. 'That was Sir Garfield Sobers.' I said.

'And what is special about him?' asked the American.

'He doesn't think he's special, that's what,' I said.

January 1996

CHARACTERS

Cec Pepper – his own man

CEC PEPPER spent most of his career in English League cricket but there was never any doubt about his roots. He was a dinky-di Aussie, a turbulent man and one of the best all-round cricketers Australia has ever produced. I base that judgement on what my eyes told me and on the evidence of Keith Miller, who rang shortly after Cec had died to say that in his view you could rank Pepper with Benaud and there were those who thought that Cec might have the edge.

Miller reckoned Pepper's flipper was the best ball he saw in his entire career. 'It skimmed off the pitch at you,' he said. Pepper, like Miller, was nobody's lapdog. Perhaps he lacked Miller's effortless charm which is why, when he had a run-in with Don Bradman in 1946, it proved to be terminal.

Pepper was a stalwart of the great Australian Services team and played against South Australia at Adelaide when Bradman made his comeback after the war years and injury. Early in Bradman's innings Pepper caught him in front and appealed for lbw. The umpire rejected the appeal whereupon Pepper asked the umpire just what a bowler had to do to get a decision against Bradman in Adelaide. The umpire reported Pepper and he was left out of the Australian team to tour New Zealand later that year. Cec packed his bags and came to England

where for the next twenty years he enlivened proceedings with his great talent and huge competitive spirit.

Pepper became one of the legendary figures in league cricket in the north of England. On one occasion, having bowled an over of leg spin, flippers and googlies at a batsman who had not the slightest idea what was happening, he said after the sixth ball, 'It's all right lad, you can open your eyes now . . . it's over.'

When he became an umpire there were those who wondered if he might curb his tongue on the field of play. He didn't. For one who suffered at the hands of officials both as a batsman and bowler he showed little sympathy for his fellow professionals once he changed sides. Before a game he was officiating at Essex, Bruce Francis, a fellow Aussie, was chatting to Cec about the season and happened to remark he had been dismissed lbw sixteen times. When Francis came in to bat he had hardly got moving before he was struck on the pad. 'That's seventeen times, Bruce,' said Cec, sticking his finger up.

Cec was playing in one match at Burnley when an amateur in the side, Derek Chadwick, ran round the boundary to catch a skier off the Australian's bowling and collided with the sightscreen.

Play was held up while Mr Chadwick was revived, giving Mr Pepper time to mull over what he considered to be a chance missed off his bowling. Some time later, with Burnley struggling, the captain asked Pepper what he should do. 'Why don't you get that lad to run into the sightscreen again, it might distract the batsmen,' said Cec.

Playing against Gul Mohammed, the Indian Test cricketer who was the professional at Ramsbottom in the fifties, Pepper totally baffled him with leg-break, top spin, flipper and googly. After one over when, in spite of extraordinary contortions, the unfortunate batsman didn't get near the ball, Pepper walked up to him and said, 'As a batsman you'd make a bloody good snake charmer.'

May 1993

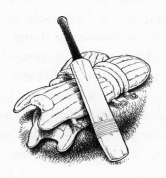

David Lloyd – class act from Accrington

IF you ask David Lloyd about his heroes he says, 'Rohan Kanhai, Ken Platt, Garfield Sobers, Jimmy James, Keith Miller and Albert Modley.' When he arrives for a *Test Match Special* broadcast his briefcase contains the *Complete Stanley Holloway Monologues*. He can do 'Albert and the Lion' without looking at the book.

As if this was not enough, he thinks that George Formby was as good an all-rounder as Ian Botham and says that, if required, he would be prepared to fill the odd twenty minutes or so entertaining the listening public with his rendition of Formby's greatest hits. He tells you this with a straight face; but, like all deadpan comedians, the eyes are crafty and humorous.

When he decided to play cricket for a living, the Wheel Tappers and Shunters Club lost a good comic. What cricket gained was a player able enough to captain his county and almost captain his country, an umpire, a coach, a first-rate commentator and a top-class after-dinner speaker.

Cricket and David Lloyd were made for each other. The accents of cricket, its class system, its folklore and, most of all, its humour, were gift-wrapped for a boy from Accrington with a God-given appreciation of the absurd.

When we say Accrington we are talking serious Lancashire. It is like Rotherham to Yorkshire, pickled onions to pork pie. When they say, 'You can take the boy out of Accrington but not Accrington out of the boy,' it gives you a fair indication of what you might expect. When the boy never bothered to leave Accrington in the first place, then you know you are dealing with the genuine article.

I dwell on David Lloyd's background because it defines his ambitions and explains his style. He believes in Lancashire as a separate land with Accrington as its capital and a population of cricket-loving humorists who sleep in pyjamas covered in red roses. The 'enemy' lives in the south and, generally speaking, is soft in the head.

When David Lloyd commentates on cricket or makes a speech, neither the bluntness of his opinions nor the plump sounds of his accent leave any doubt about where he comes from or how he was brought up.

'Tell me, Bumble, do you think Gooch should be the England captain?' asked Johnners. 'No, I don't,' said Lloyd. Watching Merv Hughes in the field: 'He's a time-bomb, ticking away, waiting to go off.' Observing Dickie Bird remonstrating with players for running on the wicket: 'They say he's a sandwich short of a picnic, that Dickie Bird. Not him. He knows what's going on. He's got all his chairs at home, has Dickie. He's saying to 'em, "Ayup, get off that pitch or else I'll have you." Doesn't miss much. Good umpire.'

It's a toss-up whether Lloyd likes commentating as

much as he liked playing the game. When you ask him he says he enjoyed being an umpire best of all. He says he gets the same thrill waking up in the morning and going to the commentary box as he did entering the pavilion as a player.

'I think about it the same way. How I'll approach the day, what I might say. I have in mind my father. He's eighty years old, cantankerous at times. He's sitting there saying, "Go on. Tell me what's happening. Entertain me."

'The other thing is being part of an institution. That's what *Test Match Special* is. Whenever I make speeches around the country I say, "If anything happens to *Test Match Special* there would be a national day of mourning," and it gets a round of applause. People care. It's part of their lives.'

He was a boy of sixteen when he came to Old Trafford. He bowled left-arm spin, unorthodox, googlies and chinamen. 'You can't bowl like that,' they told him.

Now he is Lancashire's coach the words echo down through the years. 'Coaching isn't about changing people. Am I going to change the way Wasim Akram bowls? What I have to do is give the players confidence, to get them ready to go out and play to the best of their ability.

'I think the four-day game will improve standards. It'll cut out mediocrity. The best players will come through. The raw talent is there. Lots of good young players coming through the schools system. It's more efficient than it used to be. What I'm looking for now

is a leg-spinner. Love leg-spinners. Always something might happen. Two or three bad balls then a jaffa. That's what I want to find, a leg spinner . . . [a pause] . . . an English leg-spinner.'

Lloyd's Test career lasted twelve months. He started with an unbeaten double-century against India and then came across Lillee and Thomson in 1974–75. Bill Frindall, in his book on England Test cricketers, says Lloyd had his Test career and confidence wrecked by that tour.

David Lloyd disagreed. 'Searing pace, Thomson. Their version of Tyson. Mike Denness said, "We need a left-hander at the start of our innings to take Thomson." I thought that sounded like me. Got hit in the groin. Inverted the box. Next innings got one in the throat. But all things considered, I did pretty well against them. Didn't matter. My Test career was over. But it didn't get me down. Whenever they announced a Test team and they'd picked someone else in my place, I always used to say that he got the job because he was from down south. For no other reason.'

'Does that still happen?' I asked. He gave me a withering look.

'The people who run the England cricket team all live in the south within twenty miles of each other, don't they?' he said.

Nonetheless, he might have been captain of England. He had an outside chance in 1980 when he was brought back for the one-day internationals against the West Indies.

Lloyd's account of what happened is a perfect example of his droll style. 'I was told I'd be batting number seven and if I showed up well, got a few runs and handled the quicks okay, I would be in with a chance with a couple of others when it came to the captaincy. I remember taking guard and watching Malcolm Marshall walking back to his bowling mark. I thought to myself, "I don't go that far on my holidays."

'He set off towards me. He was halfway there when I thought, "I bet he doesn't want me to play forward to this delivery." He let go this ninety miles per hour thunderbolt at me and I played what I can only describe as a very hurried backward defensive prod. The ball smashed into my forearm and broke it in two places. As I was helped from the field I remember thinking, "I wonder if I've done enough."'

Why umpiring when he gave up cricket? 'Same game, different view. When I was a player Viv Richards would whack the cricket ball and I would have to run and fetch it. As an umpire I had the pleasure of watching Viv smash the ball all round the park and some other poor beggar would run after it.

'Fascinating, too, standing when great bowlers like Hadlee or Marshall were bowling, watching them set a batsman up, then do him. Great art. Watching great art, that's what it's all about. Also, because you've played the game you're on the same wavelength. They can't try it on. If they do they must know you'll have 'em.

'I remember Bill Alley when he was umpiring, catching our bowler, Peter Lee, picking the seam. He

inspected the ball carefully, threw it back to Peter and said, "If you don't get seven for twenty with a ball like that I'll report you to Lord's."

'Some great characters, too. Arthur Jepson was a magnificent umpire and a tremendous character. He had a broad Nottinghamshire accent and a booming voice. We were playing Gloucestershire in that famous one-day game when it went pitch black. When the light was very bad Jackie Bond, our skipper, had a word with Arthur. "Light, light, what's wrong wi' t'light?" said Arthur. Bond pointed out they could barely see wicket to wicket.

'Jepson snorted dismissively. "What's that up there?" he bellowed, pointing his finger skywards. "The moon, Arthur," said Bond. "Well if tha' can see that bloody far, there can't be that much wrong wi' t'light," said Arthur. In another match, I was bowling and was half-way through an over when Arthur said, "I hope you don't mind me mentioning this but you are the worst bowler I've ever seen. Fred Price was a bad 'un, but you're worse than him."'

The folklore of cricket is in good hands so long as there are people like David Lloyd about. So is the game's pleasant nature. He is not without his critics. A Lancashire member once enquired if it could be right for someone with an accent as broad as Lloyd's to captain Lancashire. At times like that it helps to come from Accrington and be born with a sense of humour.

He doesn't please everyone on *Test Match Special*. This is not surprising since the programme's genius is to ensure such a mixture of accents and attitudes that

someone, somewhere is bound to be upset before the day is over.

I asked Peter Baxter, producer of the programme, to sum him up. 'Self-deprecating, strong-minded and frank, above all funny,' he said. That would be a fair description of him, not only as a commentator but as a cricketer, umpire, after-dinner speaker, coach and man. With David Lloyd, what you hear is what you get.

June 1993

David Lloyd has succeeded in making the homely accents of East Lancashire famous worldwide through his regular television commentaries. His enthusiasm tends to embrace the game's more radical changes – for example he has been a consistent advocate of central contracts for England players. He was England coach from spring 1996 till the completion of the 1999 World Cup.

JACK RUSSELL –
BATTLE-HARDENED PAINTER

J ACK RUSSELL says bowlers develop an extra yard of
   pace when he appears. He wonders why. Because he
gets up their noses, that's why. He is a pimple on the
face of their ambition. They didn't spend long hours
learning the art of seam and swing to run in and bowl
at this twitchy, nurdling, nicking batsman who has
devised his own eccentric method as annoying to the
opposition as it is invaluable to his team. When asked
about the qualities required to make a Test cricketer,
Raymond Illingworth talked about heart and willpower.
'Bugger technique,' he said. He would have had Jack
Russell in mind.

Watching him play for England this year has only
demonstrated what we have been missing and begs the
question why he was ever left out in the first place.
Those who know him well think he is playing better
than ever because being given the captaincy at Gloucestershire has made him both an improved cricketer
and a more amenable human being. He was always a
rum one – he is a wicket-keeper after all, and an artist
as well – but this season he has become more gregarious
and less inclined to spend time worrying about the
moment ten years ago when he dropped a catch or
missed a stumping.

When he came out to bat at The Oval, with Curtly

Jack Russell

Ambrose on a hat-trick, I was strangely reassured. More so than I would have been with any other batsman in the England side, including Michael Atherton and Graham Thorpe, both of whom can bat for my life any day of the week. Russell calmly thwarted Curtly's ambition and was then paid the dubious compliment of facing the quickest ball that Ambrose, or anyone else, bowled this year. When I asked him about it later he said, 'I think they save it up for me. I must get on their nerves.' He can say that again.

His innings at Old Trafford on the last day, when it seemed likely that we might snatch defeat from the jaws of victory, might look insignificant in the scorebook but was one of the gutsiest displays in a series that has not been short on courage and talent from players on both sides. His innings yesterday was yet another demonstration of how important he has become in Illingworth's plan for the future of English cricket.

There is not much of him, but he is a warrior. I can pay him no higher compliment. He is fascinated by battles and the deeds of brave men. It is said that when he drives to work in the morning he plays a tape of the theme tune of the Gloucester Regiment. His neat and spacious art gallery in Chipping Sodbury has paintings of the raid on St Nazaire and the Cockleshell Heroes alongside cricket scenes and portraits of Ian Botham and Don Bradman.

His interest in military matters is deep and serious. He says that the only event he would miss a cricket match for is the annual meeting of the St Nazaire

Society. When he talks about a military event he tends to give you a potted history. 'Cockleshell Heroes,' he says, talking about his picture of men in canoes. 'December 1942. Ten Royal Marines. Daring raid on enemy shipping in Bordeaux harbour. Only two survivors. Brave, brave men.'

He is fascinated by the nature of valour. He wonders if he would have the nerve to be courageous. When he plays at The Oval he spends whatever time he can at the Imperial War Museum, where he sits in the trenches that are part of the reconstruction of a battlefield in Flanders. On one occasion, he sat still for so long that visitors thought he was an exhibit and were somewhat taken aback when he came to life and went for a cup of tea.

'I know it sounds mad, but I just absorb the atmosphere and try to imagine what it must have been like for those men who went over the top knowing they had little chance of survival. It tells you something about brave men. Someone once said of Commandos that they had a "calm edge" to them. I think I'm getting to know what they meant.

'I'm not trying to make a comparison between what brave men do in war and Test match cricket. That would be stupid. But there is, nonetheless, a mental barrier which we have to go through, particularly when the quicks are charging in. No one fancies them and you have to conquer fears, real and imagined. Actually, I quite enjoy it. In cricket terms, it is the ultimate challenge. I think my team-mate Courtney Walsh bowls faster at

me than the others. He's a great bowler. Never tires, never gives up, and a complete gentleman. I think Walsh is as quick as anyone I've faced or kept to. Sylvester Clarke would be another, though what you have to understand about the best fast bowlers is that they're all capable of letting one go that's truly awesome.'

What about the generally held theory that all wicket-keepers have a slate loose? 'It's a difficult job, that's true. I suppose I can be pleased with the way things have gone for me this season, but I can't help thinking all the time of missing stumping Campbell off Illy at Trent Bridge. Knotty [Alan] rang me up and told me not to worry and that I kept better as the match went on. I keep going back to my mistake, wondering what I did wrong,' he said.

There would have been a time, not too long ago, when the post-mortem would have been held in his hotel room in solitary splendour while his team-mates relaxed with the odd beer elsewhere. It earned him the reputation of being a strange and solitary cove. He became even more remote and secretive when he started sketching cricket grounds and fellow players in the late eighties. He was untrained as an artist and uncertain of his talent. He thought that his team-mates might mock his pictures. And they did. There is less of that nowadays because he can command a fee of £12,000 for his best paintings and is capable of earning far more as an artist than he makes from cricket.

He has enough commissions to support a full-time career, but he has no thought of giving up the summer

job. Not for a while at least. 'It gets harder. There's no doubt about that. But I think I'm a better player now. I think I can last another ten years,' he says. If he does, he will have worn out his new pair of gloves. He reluctantly discarded the old pair when they fell apart after a decade of service. He had repaired them with needle and thread, glue and sticking plaster. They were battered and thread-bare but that's the way he likes them. 'I like them when the stuffing is hammered flat. I want to feel the ball,' he said. He doesn't like change. He has worn the same sun hat for fifteen years and though hairstyles come and go, Jack Russell resolutely sticks with the cut a barber gave him in the seventies.

His inspiration and mentor was Alan Knott, another who did nothing to disprove the axiom that wicket-keepers are barmy. 'I can remember the moment when I knew I had to be a wicket-keeper. It was 1977 and we were playing Australia at Headingley. McCosker was batting, Tony Greig bowling. McCosker nicked it and Knott dived in front of first slip to make the catch. I knew in that moment what I wanted to do,' he said.

This season he has re-established himself as England's first-choice wicket-keeper. He can justifiably claim to be the best wicket-keeper/batsman in the world, having a better average than either Ian Healy, of Australia, or the South African, David Richardson. On the evidence of his innings yesterday he is playing better now than at any point in his career.

It was rumoured that Ray Illingworth had his doubts about Jack Russell. Not any more. 'It was said I wasn't

his cup of tea. I think he might have changed his mind,' said Russell, with a smile.

When this season is over he can think of packing his cricket gear and sketch pad for the tour of South Africa. 'Always wanted to go there,' he said. Why? I asked. 'Rorke's Drift,' he said without hesitation.

August 1995

Jack Russell's contribution was one of the major reasons for Gloucestershire's success in one-day cricket around the turn of the century. By standing up to the wicket against faster bowlers, Russell played a key part in coach John Bracewell's tactical plan to stifle the opposition's big hitters. Russell left the international scene at the end of 1998; he played his 500th first-class innings for Gloucestershire in 2001. He continues to paint.

Phil Tufnell – a rough diamond

I f ever they were tempted to make a film about the young Arthur Daley, then Phil Tufnell should get the part. Even in his Middlesex blazer he looks like someone in pursuit of a nice little earner. He has the young/old face of a street kid, the Cockney charm of a fruit stall spieler. When he smokes he holds his cigarette in a cupped palm and his eyes are shrewd and humorous. He is aware he doesn't fit the mould of an international cricketer, particularly one who has spent his working life being inspected by the residents of Lord's. He says, 'I know I don't represent the proper image. If I didn't walk with my feet at ten to two and enjoy a fag I'd be England captain by now.'

As it is, he can't get a place in the England team, which wouldn't matter if all there was to the man had been described above. However, we are discussing our best spin bowler, who has not been picked for the England team since the Test in Adelaide last year. In that time the spin bowling has been left to cricketers with barely a ha'p'orth of Tufnell's talent. He has the ability to win a match when the pitch is helpful and to bowl line and length with teasing flight when it isn't. During a period when the performance of the England team is most charitably described as disappointing, he hasn't

Phil Tufnell

had a sniff, despite currently being the top English spinner in the first-class averages.

Raymond Illingworth put it most delicately: 'He is a good bowler who finds it difficult to fit into a team plan.' Graham Gooch observed, 'His carefree flippancy had me seething. Phil has a marvellous talent as a bowler but his mental toughness seems suspect . . . if he loses out on a decision he throws a tantrum.' The contrast between Gooch, the ultimate professional, and the maverick bowler caused the former England captain to ask Ian Chappell how to get the best out of Tufnell. The Australian said, 'Bowl him more often. That way, at least he won't be fielding.'

A former team-mate said, 'He is talented, aggressive and entertaining. He can also be a pain in the backside. There have been signs in the past twelve months he is maturing. My own view is he must be encouraged and given every chance to show he has changed. He is, when all is said and done, a marvellous bowler.'

The prejudice against Phil Tufnell is deep-seated. His tantrums on the field, particularly during five overseas tours, would have been bad enough, but he also troubled police as well as umpires. He was fined in 1994 for assaulting his former fiancée, and was beaten up by the girl's father. He was forgiven by the selectors and chosen to tour Australia but admits, with hindsight, he would have been better off staying at home. 'That was the most terrible time of my life. I was stressed and worrying all the time. I hadn't seen my daughter for a year or so. I

wasn't up to touring and should have realised it at the time,' he said.

Since returning from Australia, apart from one game as twelfth man, nothing. Not being picked to go to South Africa hurt him. Turning thirty made him think. He says it changed him overnight. 'I just woke up and felt different. If I think about it then obviously I am happier in myself. I have a new wife who really cares for me. I spend more time at garden centres than down the pub. Tufnell among the petunias. There'll be one or two of my team-mates raise an eyebrow at that. Then Ernie [John Emburey] leaving made me think more about my game. He was my mate and my teacher and I miss him. But when he left it meant I had to take more responsibility and I've enjoyed it.'

Tufnell cannot remember a time when he didn't play cricket. At the age of nine he was opening the bowling and the batting for his club's junior team. As someone who eventually batted below Devon Malcolm for England it can be assumed his bowling developed much more than his batting. He bowled medium pace until he was thirteen, when a coach showed him how to grip the ball for a leg-break and he found he could spin with ease.

When he was fourteen his mother died and he gave up cricket for two or three years. When I asked why he first said, 'I was a bit of a teenager I suppose, trying to get into pubs under-age and all that.' Then, later on, he said, 'When something like that happens in a family, things fall apart. When Mum died, going for a practice

on a Tuesday night and being shouted at by a load of blokes wasn't what I wanted.'

The troubled teenager was expelled from school and started work with his father, a silversmith. 'I was soldering up a carving trolley when Dad said, "What you doing sitting in here breathing in these fumes when you could be playing cricket? Get your arse down to Lord's." So I joined the groundstaff and I thought, "Hold on, this is a nice job wearing a blazer and all that."'

He was seventeen. The next thirteen years were eventful. Looking back, he acknowledges he wasn't a saint but asks who was. He says whenever he let himself down he did so because he was annoyed at his own performance. If he bowled badly he would lie awake at night worrying. He envied Emburey who, if he bowled a bad ball, shrugged and got on with the job of making sure the next delivery was a good one. He recalls that when he took his first Test wicket he was criticised for not shaking hands with his captain. 'Didn't see him. I was too busy celebrating the fact that my epitaph would not read: "He never got a Test wicket". It used to give me nightmares.'

I asked him if he felt he deserved his reputation as an awkward customer. 'I think I have let myself down but I also think I've been unfairly judged at times. A bit of both. On the other hand, I know I've learned a lot from my bad experiences. I've had an up-and-down sort of life but I'm happy now and feel relaxed about everything. I try to be level-headed about being ignored by the selectors. I'm not big-headed about playing. I haven't got a

right to be in the side. All I am saying is that if they stuck with me through the bad times, and they did, then maybe they ought to consider me in the good times when I have calmed down. I would like to repay their patience.'

He wants to be selected for the coming tour to Zimbabwe and New Zealand. I put it to him his reputation as a poor tourist was such it might be unlikely. 'But I don't agree I am a bad tourist. If I was, why have I been on five tours? Sixteen of my twenty-two Tests have been abroad. I think I'm a good tourist. I am one of the bubblier ones, always geeing the lads up in the dressing-room,' he said.

I told him that more practical reasons for the selectors' indifference might be a feeling he wasn't spinning the ball like he once did and his poor batting and ordinary fielding made him a luxury in the view of the current management. He said he worked hard at his fielding, and his batting had improved although there was not much danger he would score a ton.

He bridled at the reservations about his bowling. 'I spin it as much as any finger spinner in the game and nowadays I am a lot cannier. I know the game better. You have to understand cricket if you are a spin bowler. If a bloke is bowling at ninety miles per hour and another at ten, who do you think the batsman is going to tuck into?

'When I tell people I'd like to stay in the game as a coach or something they laugh. You can see them going nudge nudge, wink wink. But I'd be good at man-management because I know what it's like to be an awkward sod and understand that what is often thought of as a bad attitude is sometimes simply an attitude to win.'

What he wants more than anything is to re-establish himself as part of the England squad. There is little doubt they are less accomplished and more drab without him. He could be forgiven for thinking that there is a plot to keep him out.

'I have the feeling that somehow I'm the bogeyman not to be sat next to, that the theory is we can't pick him because he's banned from touring. I imagine them fearing I might poison the tea-lady or knife the gateman or run on to the middle at Lord's with my trousers down,' he said. He wasn't getting paranoid was he? 'A bit maybe, but I always remember my dad telling me when I was a nipper I was the kind of person who had to do twice as much as everyone else to convince people I was any good.' Only now does Phil Tufnell fully understand the truth of what his father told him.

August 1996

STYLISTS

WATCHING Chris Lewis gliding in to bowl or chasing and throwing in the outfield, I started wondering if it would make sense for cricket to take a lesson from ice dancing and offer separate marks for style. Lewis would rate the maximum. One of the joys of cricket is that more than most other games, it not only allows its participants the opportunity for artistic expression, it also encourages it.

Moreover, it is the stylists who are framed in the mind's eye. One of the first times I visited Lord's was in 1946 to see Middlesex play Somerset and even though I was not yet at secondary school, I remember clearly a tall and immaculately attired opening batsman for Middlesex leaning on the ball and gently persuading it to all parts of the field. That was my first sight of J.D. Robertson. He scored a century and even now I can see one cover drive from the bowling of Arthur Wellard with the bat flowing in a full arc as if in slow motion and the ball speeding so quickly away that it hit the boundary before Robertson had completed his follow-through.

The great K.R. Miller was the next stylist to make an impression on me. With Miller, it had as much to do with his broad shoulders, black wavy hair and natural swagger as his athleticism. No one, except perhaps Viv Richards, ever walked on to a cricket field like Miller

did. Miller looked as if he owned it, Richards as if he was about to fight for it.

I never missed a chance to watch Tom Graveney bat, and was there ever a more graceful player than David Gower? Garfield Sobers wasn't half bad and thinking of West Indians there can have been few more fulfilling sights for the connoisseur than Frank Worrell with his eye in.

Of the Australians, I always loved to watch Greg Chappell bat. If you knew nothing of his background you would swear that he had learned the game at Eton and Fenner's. The style was upright and classical in the tradition of the great post-war University batsmen such as May, Cowdrey and Dexter.

And if we are awarding marks for bowling style, there are some fine arguments to be had. I never failed to be thrilled by Fred Trueman's run-up. I still think it the best action I ever saw because not only was it graceful and passionate, it was also as technically perfect in the delivery stride as a fast bowler can be.

Lillee, storming in with the crowd chanting, was as awesome; Holding, rippling and silent like a curtain closing, was as menacing; Imran, stretched and airborne at the moment of delivery, as dramatic. But none, in my view, matched Fred. Rough-hewn he might have been, but there was a wonderful symmetry about his bowling.

I imagine it must have been a pleasure to have been bowled by Bishen Bedi. There was something almost deferential in his approach to the wicket. Any enquiry to the umpire was courtly. To be bowled by Tony Lock was like being mugged. To be dismissed by Bedi was akin to being handed a letter by a man in a frock-coat saying your services were no longer required.

I am, as you will by now be aware, on the way to picking my team of great stylists. I am missing a wicket-keeper. If a definition of style is making a difficult job look easy, then Keith Andrew is my choice; if style is making a difficult job look impossible, then Godfrey Evans would have few rivals. John Murray and Jeffrey Dujon were two wicket-keepers of great charm and elegance.

Here then is my All-Time XII for the World Style Cup:

J.D. Robertson, Barry Richards, Tom Graveney, David Gower, Greg Chappell, Garfield Sobers, Keith Andrew, Dennis Lillee, Michael Holding, F.S. Trueman, Bishen Bedi, K.R. Miller.

I am sure there are others I have overlooked. There are, of course, no absolute judgements to be made about style; except to say that it is much easier to detect than to acquire.

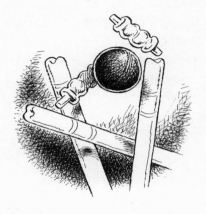

THE QUICKS

Fire and brimstone

Fast bowlers are set apart from their fellow men by a mixture of fear, envy, grudging respect and slack-mouthed admiration. In the whole of sport, only the heavyweight champion of the world commands the same clutch of reactions. They carry with them on the field of play the threat of sudden violence. They are the men who probe the taproots of technique, lay bare the nerve endings. As Maurice Leyland once observed: 'None of us like 'em, but not all of us lets on.'

Being the son of a fast bowler, I know more than a little about them. If I grew up nervous of the quickies it was only because I lived with one for a considerable length of time and although, contrary to common rumour, my old man did not eat raw meat, he undoubtedly meant business when he had a cricket ball in his hand.

Like all fast bowlers, he didn't mind whom he hit or where he hit them. Any fast bowler, if he is honest, will admit to the same attitude, and if he says different he is probably changing sex and will likely end up playing in frilly drawers with Rachel Heyhoe Flint as his captain. I am not saying that it is necessary for a fast bowler to be a homicidal maniac, but it certainly helps.

My old man was the gentlest of souls off the field, but when striding in to rocket the ball at his opponent he didn't really care whether he knocked over the batsman or the wickets.

He wasn't exactly popular in certain neighbouring villages where he left a trail of sore limbs and bruised reputations; nor was he immune from counter-attack. As a child I remember the crowd cheering as Father was carried off after being felled by the local fast bowler who repaid a broken rib from a previous encounter by hitting my old man straight between the eyes.

For a week or so thereafter he sported the most spectacular pair of black eyes outside the panda house at London Zoo. It didn't seem to bother him too much. 'I'll bet you yon fast bowler doesn't turn up at our ground,' was all he said. And he was right, the excuse being that the fast bowler's Uncle Willy had taken a turn for the worse and needed looking after.

The presence of a really fast bowler in a team has always guaranteed a selection problem for the other side. Many's the captain who has been told on the eve of a game that one or more of his batsmen have poorly grannies or upset stomachs. Speaking personally, I don't think I have ever run away from an encounter with a quick bowler, but it is also undeniably true that all my best and bravest innings against genuine pace have been played in the club bar.

I was lucky in that in all the years I have played cricket, no matter what the level or the state of the track, I have never been badly injured, which probably argues much for my technique against pace consisting as it does of playing from a position somewhat adjacent to the square-leg umpire.

Even that technique is not infallible because although

it has served me well it did not prevent one of my former opening partners getting hit on every square inch of his person. He was the most accident-prone cricketer I have ever seen.

I cannot remember one game in the three seasons I played with him when he did not suffer some disaster. And if he didn't sustain an injury in the middle he would compensate by falling off his bike going home. His injuries were so frequent and varied that the local St John's Ambulance Brigade instructor used to pick him up every Monday and take him down to the village hall to let his students practise on him.

He was known as 'WC' because of the amount of time he spent in that establishment prior to facing a quick bowler. I used to have to knock on the door to tell him it was time to go to the middle whereupon he would emerge wan and trembling to face his weekly encounter with disaster.

He wore more protection than a medieval knight and was the only player I knew who wore two groin protectors – one a lightweight batsman's job and the other a monstrous stumper's affair which covered every part of his lower abdomen.

I was present the day he was struck in that most protected part of his body by a fast bowler of immense pace. As he lay on the floor he indicated in somewhat robust terms that the blow had trapped a certain part of his anatomy between the two boxes. The bowler took the news phlegmatically enough. 'Looks like a job for t'fire brigade then,' he said.

The thought of being attended to by fire officers wearing brass helmets and wielding oxyacetylene equipment proved too much for WC, who retired to his favourite room in the pavilion in order to supervise his own emergency operation. I often wonder what went on at the local ambulance class the following Monday.

Fast bowlers make things happen because they deal in fire and spectacle. They are the flamboyant swankpots of cricket because they carry the ultimate deterrent. Often this sense of power sends them queer in the head. For instance, I knew one black quickie of fearsome pace and reputation who earned a living as a bus driver and became so convinced of his reputation as the local superman that he would not stop to pick up passengers if there was a white man at the bus stop. Thus he would often tour the town all day without stopping, his clippie snoozing contentedly on the top deck.

But generally we should forgive fast bowlers anything for they are to cricket what comets are to the heavens. Batsmen are more durable, slow bowlers have a duller and more lasting gleam, but the real speed merchants are here and gone leaving a brilliant memory trailed by a gasp of wonder.

Lillee, Thomson, Roberts and Holding of the moderns similarly light up the scene. On and off the field they are the centre of all attention, provoking that mixture of hostility and respect so peculiar to their breed. They handle the situation well because the fastest bowler in the world, like the best fighter, doesn't have to prove a thing in a street brawl.

I remember standing in a bar with Fred Trueman when a man shoved a tatty piece of paper under his nose, 'twixt pint and lips and said, rudely, 'Sign that.' Fred lowered his pint, and slowly looked the man up and down. The man got the message. 'Would you mind very much signing your autograph, please, Mr Trueman,' he said. Fred did so without saying a word.

Once, I tried the same tactic. Coming off the field from a charity game, a youth roughly grabbed my arm and stuck an autograph book under my nose. 'Put yer name on it,' he commanded. I gave him Fred's look. 'Blimey,' he said, 'yer look like my bleedin' probation officer.'

HAROLD LARWOOD
1904–95

Long before I ever met him I knew him well. My
father told me he was the greatest fast bowler that
ever drew breath and paid him the ultimate compliment
of hero worship by copying his run to the wicket. Jack
Fingleton, who also knew what he was talking about,
said he was the best fast bowler he ever faced. He was,
said Fingo, 'the master'.

Harold Larwood was a giant in my imagination, a
legendary figure whose bowling frightened the greatest
batsman there has ever been (and a few more besides)
and in doing so created a political brouhaha of such
resonance it echoes still, sixty years on.

When I first saw him, standing outside a Sydney restaurant in 1979, he looked like one of the miners who
would loiter around the pub on Sunday mornings waiting for the doors to open at midday.

He seemed uncomfortable in his suit, as if it was his
Sunday best, his trilby hat was at a jaunty angle and he
was smoking a cigarette which he cupped in the palm
of his hand as if shielding it from a wind.

He was of medium height with good shoulders and
the strong, square hands of someone who had done
some shovelling in his life as well as bowling. My father,
in heaven at the time, would have been delighted with

my impression that he and his great hero were peas from the same pod.

On the other hand, I had expected something altogether more substantial, someone more in keeping with the image I had of a man who terrorised opponents and whose fearsome reputation was such that at one moment in time governments were in thrall as he ran in to bowl.

In all of sport there never was a story to match the Bodyline saga. At its heart was the ultimate sporting challenge: a contest between the two greatest players in the world. In 1932–33 Donald Bradman was in his prime, the finest batsman of his generation, or any other before or since. Harold Larwood was also in his pomp, the fastest bowler in the world and about to prove himself the most lethal and unerring there has ever been.

The impresario of this world title contest was Douglas Jardine, the captain of England, patrician, implacable and a terrible snob who treated Australians with a contempt he never bothered to conceal. The story that unfolded around these three characters had everything except sex and a happy ending.

I was tempted to say it would have made a marvellous soap for television, except one was produced and a right mess they made of it.

The controversy stirred by Bodyline pursued Harold Larwood all his days. It changed him from a cricketer into a hunted man who hid away in a sweetshop in Blackpool before being persuaded by Jack Fingleton to seek a new life in Australia, where he ended his days

surrounded by his large family in suburban Sydney amid the accents that once denounced him as the devil.

It was Jack Fingleton and Keith Miller who arranged my meeting with Harold; Bill O'Reilly was there too, and Arthur Morris and Ray Lindwall, so you could say I was in the best of company. There were so many questions I wanted to ask but dared not lest I turned what was a friendly lunch into a press conference. In any case, in that company I was superfluous to requirements except as a witness to what happened.

We sat at a round table on a spring day in Sydney. We all drank wine except Harold who said he was a beer man. 'Always had a pint when I was bowling,' he said. 'We used to sneak it in with the soft drinks. A pint for me and one for Bill Voce. You must put back what you sweat out,' he said.

'I hope you weren't drunk when you bowled at me,' said Jack Fingleton.

'I didn't need any inspiration to get you out,' Harold Larwood replied. Jack said of all the bowlers he faced, Larwood was the fastest and had the best control.

'He was a very great bowler. Used to skid the bouncer. Throat ball,' said Jack.

Larwood took the compliment and said, 'You might not have been the best batsman I bowled against but you were certainly the bravest. I could hit you all right but you wouldn't go down. You weren't frightened, not like one or two I could mention but won't.'

Tiger O'Reilly said he was once sent out to bat against Harold when the ball was flying about, having been

instructed by his skipper to stay at the crease at all costs. He was endeavouring to follow these instructions and was halfway through his backlift when Larwood bowled him a ball he sensed but did not see. 'I felt the draught as it went by and heard it hit Duckworth's gloves,' said Tiger. Being a sensible fellow, he decided on a new method which, as he described it, involved his standing alongside the square-leg umpire with his bat stretched towards the stumps.

'It was from this position,' said Tiger, 'I was perfectly placed to observe a most extraordinary occurrence. Larwood bowled me a ball of such pace and ferocity that it struck the off bail and reduced it to a small pile of sawdust.' When I first told this story, a reader wrote to say that what O'Reilly claimed was clearly impossible. I wrote back informing the reader that O'Reilly was Irish and heard nothing more on the matter.

Jack Fingleton told Harold Larwood, 'You didn't need to bowl bodyline. You were a good enough bowler to get anyone out by normal methods.' It was the first time during our luncheon that anyone had mentioned 'bodyline'. Until then, the word had ticked away in a corner of the room like an unexploded bomb.

Harold smiled. 'I was merely following the instructions of my captain,' he said. He produced from his jacket pocket a yellow duster and unfolded it to reveal a silver ashtray. The inscription said: 'To a great bowler from a grateful captain. D.R. Jardine.' The lettering was faint from nearly fifty years of spit and polish.

Jardine was the field marshal of bodyline, Larwood

his secret weapon. Jardine was the strategist, Larwood the assassin. I think it wrong to portray Larwood as the unwitting accomplice as some have done. It underestimates his strength of character, denies his intelligence and, most of all, does not take into account his determination to show Bradman and the rest of the Aussies who the boss really was.

But whereas Jardine fully understood the consequences of what he planned, Larwood was never likely to begin to fathom the undercurrents of intrigue created by his captain's strategy. They did for him in the end.

At our lunch, Harold recalled the day in 1933 when an Australian supporter accosted him and said, 'I hope you never play cricket again.' Harold Larwood replied, 'How dare you say that when cricket is my life, my job, my livelihood?' It wasn't too long before his critic's wish was granted and Harold Larwood, who thought he had been playing cricket for a living, wondered if he might have been mistaken.

After Jardine's team had thrashed the Australians, Harold Larwood, who was injured, went home ahead of the main party. He told me he realised he was to be made the scapegoat when he arrived in London to be confronted by a mob of journalists without any help from the MCC, which left him to his own devices.

Before reaching London, after his ship had docked in France, Larwood had been joined by his Nottinghamshire captain, A.W. Carr, whom he took to be his official escort. Carr quizzed him about events in Australia and Larwood answered candidly as he would to his skipper.

It was only when they arrived in London and Harold found himself on his own that he realised Carr had been working for a newspaper.

Harold said he arrived in Nottingham by train in angry mood in the early hours of the morning, to be greeted with brass band and a hero's welcome. Ordinary cricket lovers had no time for the political arguments taking place between the governments of Great Britain and Australia. All they cared about was England bringing home the Ashes and, as far as they were concerned, the man who did the job was Harold Larwood.

He enjoyed his celebrity for a while and capitalised on it. There was talk of making a movie and he went to Gamages store in London for a week to demonstrate bodyline bowling to an admiring public. For the week of personal appearances he earned five times more than he was paid for the entire tour of Australia.

He told us that the worst moment came when he was asked to apologise for the way he had bowled. He refused. 'I had nothing to be ashamed about,' he said. He never played for England again and he had only a few more seasons with Notts. Disenchanted, he bought a shop in Blackpool and didn't even put his name above the door in case it attracted rubberneckers.

It was here that Jack Fingleton found him in 1948 and persuaded him to emigrate. Jack, who also worked as a parliamentary reporter and knew his way around the corridors of power, pulled a few strings and arranged that the prime minister of Australia, Ben Chifley, be on hand to greet Harold when he arrived.

Mr Chifley was a dinki-di Aussie with an ocker accent. After introducing the two men, Jack left them to have a natter. Ten minutes later, he was joined by the prime minister. 'He's a nice bloke but I can't understand a word he's saying,' he said to Jack. Ten minutes later, Larwood appeared. 'It was nice of the prime minister to see me, but I wish I knew what he was on about,' said Harold. So Jack Fingleton sometimes interpreted for two men who both thought they were speaking English.

Harold laughed as Jack told the tale. 'And I still haven't lost my accent,' he said. And he hadn't. 'Coming to Australia was the best thing that happened to me. I've been very happy here. I was signing in at a golf club some time ago and came to the bit where they ask you where you come from and my friend suggested I put Nottingham down in the book. I told him my home was in Sydney and pointed out I had lived in Australia longer than their best fast bowler, Dennis Lillee.'

We lunched together twice more before he became housebound because of his blindness. I called to congratulate him on being awarded the MBE in 1993. I didn't tell him it was sixty years overdue. Like elephants, the establishment have long memories and small brains. With Harold gone, only Bradman remains of the key protagonists in the bodyline story. Neither man has told the whole truth, choosing to keep to themselves what they really thought about each other.

In that sense, the story has no ending and both men will be remembered for what we don't know about

them, as they will for their deeds on the field of play. Between them, the Boy from Bowral and the Lad from Nuncargate played out a story that will forever interest lovers of cricket and social historians looking for clues about the attitudes and mores of that time.

I was lucky to meet Harold Larwood and treasure the memory. I never saw him bowl, but my father did and Jack Fingleton, too. I think Jack should have the last word. 'One could tell his art by his run to the wicket. It was a poem of athletic grace, as each muscle gave over to the other with perfect balance and the utmost power. I will never see a greater fast bowler than Larwood, I am sure of that. He was the master.'

July 1995

Harold Larwood died on 22 June 1995.

RAY LINDWALL – THE PERFECT ACTION

I WATCHED part of the 1993 Sydney Test with Raymond Russell Lindwall. He had just been interviewed at some length for the national sound archive.

I think Lindwall was the greatest fast bowler that I ever saw. I can still picture him clearly, warming up as the fielders fanned out behind the bat. His action is imprinted in my memory like the footprints he left in soft English turf.

I can still see him running in (the picture is black and white), the ball swinging through Hutton's defence, the stumps shattered. I can still hear the silence as our Len walked back to the pavilion. 'Was that a good ball, Dad?' I asked, seeking reassurance. 'It had to be,' said my father, giving it.

Later, much later, Lindwall danced a foxtrot with my wife in Sydney. 'Do you know who that was?' I said. She looked bemused. 'That was one of the greatest fast bowlers of all time,' I said.

'He does a wonderful reverse chassé,' she said.

I was never sure when Ray Lindwall was leg-pulling. He possessed the deadpan face and brain of a poker player. He had a liking for the simple things and an abhorrence of fuss or palaver. I was once in his company when he was buttonholed by a fan who stared up his nostrils and delivered a speech about the joy he had

derived from a lifetime of watching the great man play cricket. It was well meant but too long and tedious. Ray listened patiently and then said, 'This cricketer you are talking about must have been a helluva player.'

He was. Anyone who watched him or faced him would not hesitate in picking him to lead the attack in their Best Ever XI. Denis Compton said he was the supreme fast bowler. John Warr, the former Middlesex and England bowler, said if he was granted one wish before he died it would be to see Lindwall opening the bowling in a Test at Lord's.

It would be difficult to convince the young visitor to Brisbane or Sydney that the man sitting quietly in the corner, drink in hand, had once both terrorised and defeated the greatest batsmen in the world. But then Lindwall never did give much away.

January 1991

Ray Lindwall died on 22 June 1996

Fred Trueman – truth and fiction blend with eloquent ease

I HAVE to tell you Fred Trueman will not be well pleased with his BBC obituary. In fact, if it appears in its present form there is every chance he will haunt Broadcasting House. In it the writer describes his action as 'lolloping'. This is a bit like saying an oak tree is 'fragile' or the flight of a swallow 'ungainly': it is the very opposite of the truth.

Before I tell you what it was like watching Fred Trueman bowl I had better explain that I came across his obituary not because he has secretly passed away – he couldn't do anything quietly – but because in researching an interviewee I sometimes see a preview of the obituary. I am glad I did on this occasion because I am able to right a great wrong.

Anyone who believes I am being pernickety never saw Fred bowl. To do so was to understand that his action was a statement both of the man and the cricketer. The walk back to his mark, the bandy-legged, broad-beamed swagger, the arrogant display of wide shoulders and muscular forearms was a crude declaration of a formidable physical presence. When he turned you would not have been surprised had he pawed the ground.

As it was, after the first few accelerating strides, he

glided rather than ran to the wicket and with his final, fulminating stride, left arm thrown high, the perfectly side-on stretch of his body described the arc of a bow. It was the action not simply of a great fast bowler but also a purist with a proper reverence for the game's style and artistic possibilities.

Fred Trueman might have made a reputation out of being a tough-talking, rumbustious Yorkshireman but his genius as a bowler was built on a technique of classical foundation. Cricket is a side-on game. Len Hutton defined the principle as a batsman, Trueman as the bowler. Fred thinks Len Hutton was the greatest batsman he ever saw and has never tired of saying so.

He is equally indefatigable expressing the opinion that the trouble with modern bowlers is they ignore basic principles. Many think he bangs on too much about such things. Maybe, except what he says is indisputably true and, what is more, no one is more entitled to speak on such matters than Frederick Sewards Trueman.

He has set down his thoughts on the game in an audiotape called *Owzat!* He tells the story of batting with Len Hutton against Gloucestershire when he hung about long enough to see the great man score a century. The opposition tried their best to get Fred to the striker's end but Hutton's ability to take a single whenever he wanted frustrated them. So they gave Len a juicy full toss to hit for four. He stroked it through the covers and set off running. The Gloucester skipper shouted to the cover fielder to let the ball go for four. As Len passed

Fred he said, 'Run three. It won't reach the boundary.' And it didn't.

Fred didn't always see eye to eye with Hutton, but he never queried his talent. Similarly, Hutton never doubted that the belligerent, chippy young man had it in him to be a very good Test bowler. As it was, Fred Trueman proved him wrong. He became a great fast bowler, arguably the best ever produced by this country and among the best half-dozen of all time.

Many years ago I was asked to write Fred's biography. I contacted the great man and agreed a deal but didn't follow through because there was too much happening in both our lives at that time for us to settle down and write the book. Eventually, John Arlott produced *Fred, Portrait of a Fast Bowler*. When I talked to John I asked how he had managed to pin Fred down. 'Didn't bother talking to him. I had seen him play. What could be more eloquent than that,' said John.

While I was still discussing the possibility of the book with Fred, we considered a title. I told Fred it should be snappy and to the point. He thought for a minute and then said, 'What about "Fred Trueman: T'Definitive Volume on T'Best Fast Bowler That Ever Drew Breath".' It is now an oft-repeated anecdote, but one I can vouch for.

On that very subject, I asked Fred how many of the stories told about him are true. He said very few. But on the other hand, strange things did happen to him. I asked him for an example and he told me of a bizarre incident which happened during a tour of India for the

Royal Cricket Association's Silver Jubilee matches. As Fred told it, he was making a long and never-ending journey by rail when the train made an unscheduled stop in the middle of nowhere and Fred alighted to be met by the station master.

He was overjoyed at meeting the famous bowler and almost beside himself when Fred asked if there was a handy toilet. He escorted Fred through the station into a room where he drew back a red velvet curtain to reveal a Victorian chamber pot mounted on a plinth. What is more, the pot had the legend 'F.S. Trueman' painted on it.

Now how it came to be there, how on earth the station master knew that Fred would one day arrive on his doorstep in need of a pee, what has since happened to such a significant piece of cricket memorabilia are important questions, but not as significant as the possibility that Fred Trueman might be adding to his own myth. When I asked him if he was being fanciful he said, 'How could I possibly make it up?'

He was, of course, the most famous quick bowler of them all. They are the gunslingers of cricket, the fastest men in town, and as such are invested with the reputation and the legend of their breed. But none has so spectacularly pursued both the romance and the reality of being a fast bowler as Fred Trueman. Like Noel Coward in another branch of the entertainment industry, he has an anecdotal history in which truth and fiction are so intertwined it is impossible to tell one from the other.

The Australian cricketer Norm O'Neill tells a story of sitting with Fred in the lounge of a Bombay hotel and saying to him, 'Fred, I believe those two Indians at the next table are talking about you.' To which Fred replied, 'Aye, Norman, they talk about me all over t'world.' Richard Hutton was once listening to Fred describing a spell of bowling in which, typically, every delivery seamed, swung and bounced, when he said, 'Tell me, Fred, did you ever bowl a ball that merely went straight?' Ignoring the barb Fred said, without hesitation, 'Aye, three years ago. It were a full toss. It went through Peter Marner like a streak of piss and knocked his middle peg out.' Peter Marner later confirmed the story although he thought it likely Fred didn't mention that it was on a dark day at Bramall Lane with him bowling at the end which didn't have a sightscreen.

I always thought that Fred Trueman bowling at Bramall Lane defined Yorkshire cricket. Some grounds greet you with a smile. Bramall Lane scowled a welcome. It wasn't pretty, but like Fred Trueman it had a certain grandeur. It wasn't even functional. Had it been so it wouldn't have had a sightscreen stuck in the middle of the football pitch and a few thousand spectators risking piles and worse by parking their backsides on terracing.

It wouldn't do nowadays but when I first knew it during the forties and fifties it fittingly represented the industrial landscape I grew up in. The same area produced Fred Trueman and to see him marking out his run at the soccer-pitch end and then come racing in with

30,000 spectators willing him on was to experience the perfect symmetry between a fast bowler and the clay that shaped him.

It was significant Fred Trueman chose Bramall Lane for his swansong in 1968. Twenty years, 2,301 wickets and 16,000 overs after first playing for Yorkshire he captained the county against the Australians. Typically, he wrote the perfect script. He scored runs, took a blinding diving catch in the gully to get rid of Doug Walters and skippered Yorkshire to a famous victory by an innings and 60 runs. Most unforgettably of all, he bowled for the last time off his long run. He was thirty-seven years of age and past his prime but what was still apparent as he ran in to bowl was what John Arlott described as 'the mounting glory of rhythm, power and majesty'.

You could see what as shrewd a judge as Trevor Bailey meant when he wrote: 'On all pitches and in all conditions it is doubtful whether there has ever been a more complete fast bowler.' It was Bailey who also supplied the archetypal Trueman anecdote. Playing against him on a fast pitch at Leyton, Trevor went to hook, missed and was sweded. When he picked himself up he found himself face to face with Fred. 'Sorry, Trev lad,' said Fred. 'There's many more I would rather have hit than thee.'

Since his retirement from the game the legend has been propagated in a never-ending stream of public appearances and after-dinner speeches. He survived major illness and even overcame a spell when Raquel

Welch was his daughter's mother-in-law. 'My run-up lasted longer,' he says.

The sadness in retirement has been his falling out with the Yorkshire County Cricket Club to the point where he says, 'I want nothing to do with them.' There is fault on both sides and a great deal of posturing and false pride at work but it is a sorry state of affairs when the most famous cricket club in the world and their most renowned bowler ignore each other.

There has also been a tendency of late, particularly among young bucks, to treat Fred as some kind of joke figure. To an extent he has himself to blame because of a tendency to expound the idea that cricket finished when he stopped playing and today's cricketers wouldn't have been employed in his day. There are times when he seems sour, discontented and out of touch: a bitter caricature of the glorious athlete that was. Perhaps it is because he was a fast bowler rather than a cricketer, part of a troublesome, quarrelsome breed; an awkward cuss.

In the end, of course, none of it matters because Fred Trueman will be judged as a player and not a personality, and as such will take his place in the pantheon. He will be at home for he has always been one for myths and deities.

I once asked him for his opinion on Yorkshire cricket and how it might escape the doldrums (this was sometime ago when Fred was still involved with the club). 'It will get better,' said Fred. He searched for the fine phrase and then said, 'Take this down, Parky lad. Fred

Trueman says, "One day Yorkshire cricket will arise like a Spartacus from the ashes".'

November 1996

With predictable panache, Fred now plays the role of a country squire in Upper Airedale. He is a regular churchgoer, supporter of good causes and in much demand as an after-dinner speaker. He remains a regular broadcaster on Test matches.

LILLEE AND THOMSON

L ILLEE and Thomson were the fire and brimstone of fast bowlers. Like all the best practitioners of their craft they tested the very limits of an opponent's nerve and technique. Add to that 50,000 people chanting their names or 'Kill . . . Kill . . . Kill' as they ran in to bowl and you begin to have a vague idea of the sort of terror gripping their opponents, who had already been told by Ian Chappell in the most direct possible manner which part of their anatomy was about to be knocked off.

They came together in 1974–75 against an England side led by Mike Denness. In the first Test, on an under-prepared wicket in Brisbane, Thomson bowled with such speed and venom that Keith Miller, sitting in a commentary box, said, 'Tommo even frightened me and I was 200 yards away.' Colin Cowdrey was sitting at home watching the mayhem on television and thinking 'rather them than me' when he received a phone call asking him to report for duty. A few days short of his forty-second birthday he found himself facing Dennis Lillee and Jeff Thomson on a bouncy track in Perth.

Out in the middle he introduced himself to Thomson and shook his hand. This confused Thomson for a moment but didn't stop him plastering Cowdrey with bouncers. He wasn't the only veteran having a hard time. Fred Titmus went out to bat and propped forward to the first ball he received from Thomson, which,

Dennis Lillee

according to Fred, pitched on a length and took his cap off. At least he thinks that is what happened because he didn't actually see the ball.

In his autobiography, Mike Denness gave a graphic account of the way the two fast bowlers frayed the nerves of the batsmen. Describing David Lloyd returning to the dressing-room after facing Lillee and Thomson, Denness wrote: 'Within seconds of his dismissal the whole of Lloyd's body was quivering. His neck and the top half of his body, in particular, were shaking. He was shellshocked ... the reaction from his continual ducking and weaving to get out of the firing line.'

In that series Thomson took 33 wickets and Lillee 25. Between them they took 555 Test wickets (Lillee 355, Thomson 200) and created a reputation which lasts to this day. At present they are reunited in a travelling talk show which is a cocktail of rumbustious anecdote and frank opinion. You can hear the authorised version on BBC Radio 5 Live on the eve of the Lord's Test. They are also here as part of the *Daily Telegraph*'s initiative to unearth a young fast bowler who will be given special coaching sessions by Lillee.

Anyone who finds it hard to believe two Australians would bother helping the Poms would do well to recall Arthur Mailey's comment when asked why he spent time discussing the intricacies of spin bowling with his opponents. Mr Mailey told his critic, 'Spin bowling is an art and art is universal.' Not that Messrs Thomson and Lillee would be so pretentious. What they believe is fast bowlers, whether they be born in Bradford,

Brisbane or Barbados, are a different species and as such should be protected. What is more, it takes one to know one.

Sometimes it is uncomfortable to meet retired warriors. It is like observing a mangy lion behind bars in a zoo. While it would be inaccurate to claim Lillee and Thomson nowadays are capable of exuding the menace of their heyday, there is still about them a formidable presence. Lillee has lost his pelt but he is broad-shouldered and barrel-chested and still slim enough round the hips to wear jeans without his belly flopping over the belt buckle. Jeff Thomson's hair is now streaked with age as well as the sun but he has the physical set-up and the stance of a decent light-heavyweight.

What made them formidable was their different approach to the same job. Lillee's run to the crease was long and dramatic in its acceleration and gathering menace. In the delivery stride the left arm was cocked, the head still and aimed down the wicket with the left shoulder as the sight. Thomson by comparison ambled to the crease but in the delivery stride the casual was transformed into the dramatic.

Lillee says that he worked on his fitness and technique and whatever reward he gained was through hard work. Thomson, on the other hand, was a freak of nature. Asked about the secret of bowling fast he said, 'Aw, I just trot in and let it go.' According to Lillee that is exactly what he did.

They first came across each other in a state game in Queensland. Lillee was the sheriff, Thomson Billy the

Kid. When Lillee came in to bat Thomson bounced him and hit him painfully on the hand. Lillee came down the wicket. 'I hope you can look after yourself when it's your turn to bat,' is a loose translation of what he said. Thomson told him to mind his own business (another approximate translation of what was actually said).

Lillee knew he had found a soulmate. He said, 'I used to love standing close in when Tommo was bowling. You could see the fear in their eyes. The psychology of fear is an important ingredient in fast bowling.' As Maurice Leyland once famously observed, putting the batsman's point of view: 'None of us likes it but not all of us lets on.'

Though different in style, both Lillee and Thomson share the same hero, Fred Trueman. Tommo says, 'I loved the way he got up the batsman's nose. He was a ratbag.' Lillee admired him for his thrilling approach to the wicket, his classic style in delivery stride and, more than anything, the way he was able to swing and seam the ball so that even when his flame began to subside he remained a constant problem to even the very best cricketers.

Similarly, Lillee was the complete fast bowler, able to sustain a career well past the time when most of his breed were retired. He reckons the time he spent playing for Haslingden in the Lancashire League was crucial. It taught him to bowl a fuller length and swing the ball away from the bat.

Thomson came to England at the tail end of his career and played for Middlesex. Incensed at being left out of

the Australian team to tour England in 1981, he made his point by flattening Graeme Wood, the Australian opener, when the tourists played Middlesex at Lord's.

It was only when he found himself egged on by his team-mates to do even more damage to the Australian team, that he realised what he had done and told them if they wanted to put any more of his former team-mates in hospital they must make their own arrangements.

Neither man has a good word for county cricket. Thomson says he enjoyed playing for Middlesex but his enthusiasm was not shared by the other players, who seemed bored by the routine of the county circuit. Lillee, who had a season with Northamptonshire, made much the same observation.

What he found most disturbing was the lack of cricket in English schools. During an enforced lay-off because of injury he made it known he was available to coach children. He had six pupils in a month. He hopes there will be a better response to their search for a fast bowler. We shall see.

The two of them will make a noisy and robust contribution to the cricket this summer. All else apart they are giving their opinions on *Test Match Special* and if they are expressed in the forthright manner employed at Lord's the other day Mrs Whitehouse will have a fit. The rest of us will have a laugh.

For all their larrikin reputation they share a ripe sense of humour. Thomson was the man who greeted David Steele when he made his way to the wicket on his England debut with the words, 'Cripes, they've picked

bloody Groucho Marx.' It was Lillee who had a Sussex batsman plumb lbw with a ripe apple and who gave Dickie Bird a sweater concealing a rubber snake. Mr Bird was over the fence and on his way to the gate when he was finally caught and persuaded back to the middle.

Anyone who saw them bowl will never forget them. Anyone who meets them now will remember why.

May 1997

MICHAEL HOLDING –
WHISPERING DEATH

THE sight of Michael Holding gliding in to bowl was one of the great aesthetic spectacles in all of sport, unless you happened to be the batsman he was running towards, in which case you were more concerned with survival than any appreciation of a great athlete in action. He ran with such style and balance be seemed to float over the turf.

Dickie Bird said he was disconcerting to work with because you couldn't hear him approaching the wicket. 'You can hear most bowlers pounding up, grunting and snorting. But often I'd stand there when Michael was bowling my end and wonder where he had got to. And then he'd flow past me like a ghost. "Whispering Death" I called him,' said Dickie.

Today, Michael Holding looks as lean, trim and stylish as ever he did when he was part of what must rate as the deadliest quartet of fast bowlers ever assembled in one team: Roberts, Holding, Garner and Croft. There have been other combinations – mainly West Indian – but none containing four bowlers of such class and ruthlessness, nor four practitioners of the same craft offering so many different ways to test the technique and nerve of their opponents.

Nowadays Michael Holding observes the game he adorned from the commentary box, his comments made

in a voice so deep and rich it sounds as if his vocal chords have been soaked in molasses. When you first meet him you are struck by the thought that he doesn't seem brutal enough to be a frightener. His manner is affable and languid and he has the most beautiful hands with long tapering fingers, like his great hero Muhammad Ali.

He told me he loved the fight game until he sat ringside for the first time. What he hadn't counted on was the noise made by leather hitting flesh. He has never been to a boxing match since. This sensitivity to human suffering will come as news to one or two of his opponents, most notably Brian Close and our new selector, John Edrich, who received a terrifying mugging from Holding, Wayne Daniel and Andy Roberts at Old Trafford in 1976.

Holding was warned by umpire Bill Alley for intimidatory bowling and Clive Lloyd, the West Indian captain, was forced to admit that his men did get 'carried away a bit'. When Close bared his chest for the cameras you couldn't quite see the ball maker's name on his flesh, but the seam marks were very noticeable. It was a severe test of Brian's theory that there is no such thing as pain.

I asked Michael Holding if he had ever deliberately set out to hurt an opponent. 'There were two names in my book of players I didn't like and I gave them both a bit of trouble,' he said. Who were they? He wouldn't say, although I have a shrewd idea that one of them might have been Tony Greig whose boast that he would

make the West Indians 'grovel' must rate along with General Custer's statement that he couldn't see any Indians as one of the most unfortunate observations of all time.

It was during that 1976 tour when the West Indies beat England 3–0 that Michael Holding produced one of the greatest Test-match bowling performances of all time. At The Oval, in the final Test on a lifeless wicket, he took 8 for 92 in England's first innings of 435 and won the match by taking 6 for 57 and bowling England out for 203 in the second innings. Holding's bowling was a classic demonstration of how great fast bowlers win matches on pitches offering nothing but heartache to less gifted practitioners. In that series Michael Holding took 28 wickets at just over 12 apiece.

It tells you much about this remarkable athlete that the performance at The Oval is not the one most people talk about when they discuss Holding's place in the all-time list of great fast bowlers. If he did nothing else, he will be remembered for one over he bowled at Geoffrey Boycott in Barbados on the England tour of 1980–81. In the folklore of cricket, those six balls have acquired the reputation of the most lethal over ever delivered. It is not something you can prove except to say that anyone who witnessed what happened, as I did, is bound to say they never saw anything quite like it.

Boycott admits he still has nightmares about that over. Holding smiles at the memory and says, 'If you believe Geoffrey, England would have been six wickets down without scoring had he not been batting.' The man

who had the best view was Graham Gooch, Boycott's partner. Gooch recalls that the first five balls were virtually unplayable, throat balls which followed Boycott as he swayed out of line. The sixth ball was pitched up and sent Boycott's off stump flying. 'It was one of the most lethal, enthralling overs I have ever seen. Classic fast bowling from a very great bowler,' said Gooch.

He remembered with a smile dear old Ken Barrington's advice as he and Boycott prepared to go out and bat in that match. He told them, 'You have just got to go steadily through them swing doors, walk calmly up to the reception desk and book yourselves in for bed and breakfast.'

I asked Michael Holding who was the fastest bowler he faced. 'Without doubt Jeff Thomson. When we toured Australia in 1975–76 he was awesome. He was the only bowler I saw who could make Lawrence Rowe play a hurried shot. How quick? Well, let's say he could have hit me any time he wanted. I just couldn't see him.' Holding was never in any danger of being injured by Thomson because in those days the Fast Bowlers Club operated, which guaranteed that the quick men did not do damage to each other.

When Fred Trueman was in his pomp (now there was an action) it was unthinkable that when he batted he would receive a short-pitched delivery. Indeed, Fred's first move at the wicket was a firm step forward. Nowadays that would guarantee him a bed in the nearest casualty ward.

There is a famous story about Fred going out to face

a young quick bowler who was making his debut and who had been wound up by his captain to bounce him just for fun. The young bowler, having more testosterone than sense, took up the challenge and whistled three balls past Fred's head. The great man was mortified. At the end of the over he approached the fast bowler. 'Tell me, young man,' said Fred, 'does tha' want to die young?'

May 1995

VIEWS ON THE GAME

TALES WORTH TELLING

A<small>T</small> the very beginning of *Close of Play*, by Neville Cardus, there is a cartoon by that talented man, Bernard Hollowood. It shows two boys standing before a wall with stumps chalked on it. One is a ragamuffin, the other bespectacled and bookish. The latter is saying to the rapscallion, 'No, you be Len Hutton. I'll be Neville Cardus.'

Although my eyesight is perfect, and not even my best friend could describe me as widely read, I have always associated myself with the bookworm in the cartoon. I wouldn't have minded being Len Hutton, but I would have sold my soul to have been blessed with Sir Neville's gifts.

I still find it difficult to believe his confession that most of those marvellous quotes he attributes to the cricketers he wrote about were invented. And yet I was prepared to do so because I heard the same statement from his own lips the one and only time I met him.

We lunched together, and because at the time I was gathering material for an article about Wilfred Rhodes, I asked him the source of one of my favourite anecdotes about Wilfred which Sir Neville had written. The story concerns Charles McGahey, the old Essex player, going out to bat on a sunny day at Bramall Lane, Sheffield. As he walked out to face Rhodes the weather changed. Looking over his shoulder at the darkening sun and

anticipating a sticky wicket, McGahey said, 'Ullo! McGahey caught Tunnicliffe bowled Rhodes . . . O.' And so it was, both innings.

Sir Neville smiled at the memory and then said, disarmingly, 'Oh, I made it up.' It was my first traumatic experience. He went on to explain that his job was to write scripts for the cricketers who, in the main, were unable to say what they undoubtedly would have said had they possessed Sir Neville's imagination. As he expounded his theory, he must have seen the look of disappointment on my face.

'You mustn't worry, young man, because it happens to be true,' he said.

'What was true?' I asked, somewhat baffled.

'McGahey caught Tunnicliffe bowled Rhodes both innings,' said Sir Neville, as if that explained everything.

Sir Neville's confession raises the whole question of the validity of the sporting anecdote. I once asked Fred Trueman, who has been the subject of more stories than any cricketer in the history of the game, how many were true. 'About ten per cent,' he said.

He didn't mind the majority of them – indeed, he was flattered – but there were one or two he could do without. The story he really objected to, and has spent a lifetime trying to deny, was the one about him sitting next to a high dignitary of the Indian government at dinner, digging him in the ribs and saying: 'Ayup Gunga Din, pass t'salt.'

All that Fred's denials have achieved is another punchline to the story whereby the teller states that when asked about the yarn's validity, Fred said, 'It's

a lie. I never said that. It were t'chutney I were after.'

Although that particular story was an original in that it was invented especially for Fred, quite a few of the others he inherited from the folklore of fast bowlers. The one about Fred objecting to a 'fancy hat' cocking a toe at him and, after sufficient warning, dropping a 90 m.p.h. yorker on the offending article, was told about Kortright, as well as Larwood, before Fred inherited it.

In the Kortright version, the bowler is alleged to have told the batsman that he allowed only one batsman to lift his toe at him, and that was W.G. Grace. The batsman declined the advice and was carried from the field.

In the Larwood/Trueman version, the stricken batsman falls to the floor in anguish. Fieldsmen gather round and remove pad, sock and boot and solicitously massage the bruised foot. After much palaver, the batsman is able to replace his gear and stand up. As he picks up his bat and prepares to continue, Harold/Fred, who has been watching the performance says, 'Are tha' alreet young feller?'

'Yes, thank you very much,' says the batsman.

'Can tha' walk?'

'I think so, thank you.'

'Good. Well, get thissen off to t'pavilion because tha'rt lbw,' says Harold/Fred.

A lovely story, but Fred denies it, and I'll bet it never happened to Larwood nor to Kortright. It doesn't really matter because as Sir Neville always believed, cricketers should concentrate on what they do best and leave the legends to those whose job it is to invent them.

THOSE WHO STAND
AND SERVE

I REMEMBER my first umpire well. His name was Jim Smith and he always took his teeth out before a game. I never discovered why but I always supposed it was a safety precaution due to the state of our wickets and the ferocity of our cricket.

He was a marvellous man, tall and dignified even without his teeth, with an infallible technique for puncturing swollen heads. I remember as a youngster playing well and scoring 50 or so in a game he was umpiring. I carried my bat and as I came off the field, triumphant, imagining myself to be an unbelievable mixture of Bradman and Hutton, he joined me at my shoulder. As we walked in together, I looked towards him anticipating a word of praise. He glanced sidelong at me and out of the corner of his mouth said, 'Does tha' want some advice, lad?'

I said I did.

'Well get thi' bloody hair cut,' he said.

Two matches later he gave me out lbw and as I walked sullenly past him he said, out of the same corner of his toothless mouth, 'If tha'd get thi' bloody hair cut tha'd stop them balls wi' thi' bat.'

Jim Smith was my introduction to that delightful body of men, the cricket umpire. I can think of no other group that does so much for so little. By comparison the soccer

referee is a pampered ninny, and the fact that cricket has survived this far without requiring the umpires to take the field carrying truncheons says much for their character. The secret, of course, lies in their humour. There are few funny stories about soccer or rugby referees and anyone who tells me a funny about a tennis umpire will receive a gold-plated pig by return of post. But there is a Bumper Fun Book of Funny Umpire Stories.

Many of them concern Alec Skelding. My favourite Skelding story concerns the aggrieved batsman who, on being given out lbw, addressed Skelding thus:

'Where's your white stick, umpire?'

'Left it at home,' said Alec.

'What about your guide dog? said the batsman.

'Got rid of it for yappin' same as I'm getting rid of you,' replied Skelding.

Joe Hayes never rose to Skelding's heights in cricket but in the local league I played in as a youth he was just as big a legend. Those who knew Joe well always appealed for everything as opening time approached because Joe had a job as a waiter in a local boozer and had to be on duty at 6 p.m. It was his proud boast that he had never been late at the boozer in twenty years, and he could produce several hundred cursing batsmen to bear him witness. His other quirk was a dislike of loud appealing. He himself rarely raised his voice above a murmur and his face creased in pain and disgust whenever a bowler bellowed in his earhole.

We had in our team at the time the best appealer of

all time. His voice rattled windows several miles away
and set dogs to whimpering. This particular game his
raucous appeals eventually got on Joe's nerves. After
one particularly loud one Joe could stand it no longer.

'Owz-that!' bellowed the bowler.

'Not out,' Joe bellowed back in an even louder voice.
The bowler stood amazed that Joe should raise his voice.

'I'm only bloody askin' thi',' he said in a pained tone.

'Ay, and I'm only bloody tellin' thi',' shouted Joe.

All of which leads to Cec Pepper, who as a player in
the Lancashire League was renowned as much for his
verbal battles with umpires as he was for his cricketing
prowess.

Pepper was the scourge of Lancashire League
umpires, blasting the meek with his belligerent appealing, making the lay preachers blush with his vivid language. The umpire who faced up to him had to be a
special kind of human being and George Long was such
a man.

George was standing one day at the end where Pepper
was bowling, when Pepper made one of his raucous
Australian appeals for lbw, which was answered by a
quiet 'Not out.' Whereupon Pepper gave vent to a his-
trionic stream of invective, throwing in all the stock-
in-trade props – spectacles, white stick, guide dog, illegitimacy, bloody-minded Englishness, and four-letter
words – all of which George completely ignored.

The same thing happened after the next ball and yet
again after the following one, after which George called
'Over' and walked to his square-leg position, followed

by Pepper – obviously disturbed by the lack of reaction from the umpire.

'I suppose you're going to report all this bad language to the League?' said Pepper.

'No,' replied George. 'Ah likes a chap as speaks his mind.' Pepper was obviously delighted.

'So do I,' he said smiling, 'and I must say it's a refreshing change to meet an umpire like you. I'm glad that we understand each other.'

'Aye,' said George.

The first ball of the next over again hit the batsman's pad, whereupon Cec whirled round to George, arms outstretched and did his usual Red Indian war whoop. His 'Owzat' was heard all round the ground.

'Not out, you fat Australian bastard,' said George quietly.

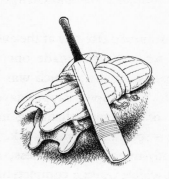

COMMENTATORS

THERE is little doubt that the Australian television coverage of the Test matches is technically streets ahead of anything British television offers. The same cannot be said about the commentary.

I have two main objections: the commentators talk too much; and much of what they say is twaddle. There are exceptions. They are called Richie Benaud and Geoffrey Boycott. Benaud has been perfecting his craft for years. Today he sets the standard for the rest to follow. Boycott, who has never been frightened of seeking good advice, is a willing pupil. There are one or two others who could do with a lesson.

Max Walker, for instance, is an affable and talented man but I do wish that occasionally he would put a cork in it. I do not wish to be informed as a bowler walks back to his mark that his heart is pounding, his mouth is dry and he is wearing size 11½ boots.

Max, by the way, is indisputably clairvoyant. He tells us that, as the bowler approaches the wicket, he will already have licked his fingers and wrapped them around the seam prior to ripping them over the top of the ball to produce the perfect leg-cutter.

Similarly, the feuds between commentators – Greig needling Lawry, Chappell needling anyone within hailing distance – sound awkward and false, like theatrical contrivance. And here's the nub: the Aussies are not so

much reporting the game as selling it like washing-up liquid.

They start from the premise that the viewer knows nothing other than the basic fact that one player throws a ball at another who tries to hit it with a piece of wood. There is nothing wrong with instructing the client provided that, after a while, you assume they have got the drift and are ready for a more sophisticated approach. Sadly, there is no room for nuance.

The producers work on the theory that if nothing is happening on the field of play – which is to say that the run rate has fallen below six an over – then the viewer must be protected from becoming bored by a series of sideshows. These range from flogging books, to cut-aways of pretty girls (known in the trade as 'crumpet shots'), to asking viewers to phone in an answer to the question of the day.

This last ploy gives a pertinent clue to the kind of thinking dominating the television presentation. The two questions posed to viewers were: should umpires make use of television technology in making decisions and should Test matches be played under lights? In other words, should television be given an even firmer stranglehold on the future of the game?

The trouble with the big sell is that, generally speaking, it creates an appetite for a certain kind of cricket: confrontational, disputatious, muscular, uncomplicated. These characteristics have their place in cricket; think of Ian Botham.

What is missing are the ingredients that make cricket

such a special game – elegance, grace, wit, even eccentricity; think of David Gower.

Most of all, it denies the viewer those contemplative moments between overs when cricket lovers see the field as a chess board and ponder the next move. In Australia there is a commercial break at the end of every over. So it is possible to go from the glory of Mark Waugh's strokeplay straight to a commercial for cockroach repellent.

Amid much that is crassly commercial, it is remarkable that Messrs Benaud and Boycott manage to be intelligent, instructive, perceptive and, above all, properly neutral. So far, Bill Lawry has refrained from appealing on behalf of the Australian bowlers, but only just. On the second day of the current Test match he did say 'That's out' when Graham Gooch was struck on the pad and before the umpire had time, quite properly, to turn down the appeal.

What Richie Benaud has accomplished, and Boycott is moving towards, but most have yet to learn, is that while a camera might show you the face of cricket only a commentator can describe its true nature.

January 1991

John Arlott – the voice
of cricket

John Arlott said, 'Meet me at the Grace Gates and we will watch Middlesex play your lot and drink a decent claret.' And we did. Fred bowled fast which always made John thirsty. I think we had a gentle kip in the afternoon and later, in the bar, I said it had been a perfect day and wasn't I the luckiest man in the world because I was paid to watch cricket and interview Rita Hayworth.

John thought a bit about this and then said he thought he had the better job because the *Guardian* paid him to watch cricket and drink wine. He told me he once had a similar conversation with Neville Cardus who said, 'But my dear John, I am a much more fortunate fellow than you.' John asked how that could be. 'Because,' said Neville, 'the *Guardian* pay me to watch the cricket and go to the opera and upon mature reflection I would rather sleep with a soprano than a wine merchant.'

That was before the melancholy set in with John. It was upsetting for his many friends that later in his life he seemed remote from the genuine love and respect they had to offer. His was a unique contribution to a game and for all he gave cricket poetic imagery and romance, he remained clear that it was only a game.

He maybe would have wished for a career in politics, something more substantial perhaps than commentating

John Arlott

on cricket. Yet, as he once told me, 'Politics governs everything we do, the games we play, the way we play them, who we play. Politics controls life because politics is the philosophy by which you live, exist and behave.'

That being the case, John Arlott influenced more people than most, not just about a game, but about the eternal verities of beauty, companionship and, above all, humour. He didn't just commentate on cricket, he told us an awful lot about ourselves.

John Arlott died on 14 December 1991 on Alderney.

DICKIE BIRD – AN UNLIKELY ICON

To say Dickie Bird loves cricket doesn't get anywhere near describing exactly what he feels for the game. It's a bit like saying that Romeo had a slight crush on Juliet or Abelard had a fancy for Héloïse.

The game consumes his life and defines its horizons. It shapes the very posture of the man.

Like a tree bent and moulded by the prevailing wind, so the curve in Bird's spine, the hunch of his shoulders, the crinkled eyes as he inspects the world, have been sculpted through a lifetime's dedication to cricket.

He is, nowadays, one of the landmarks of the game – an umpire as famous as any superstar, as much respected by cricketers as he is loved by the public.

In a few days' time, just before his sixtieth birthday, he flies to the West Indies to stand in three Tests against Pakistan. His presence has been requested by both sides. In any situation this would be a feather in his cap, but given that this is for the unofficial championship of the world, and taking into account the fierce arguments on the subject of neutral umpires, Dickie Bird could be forgiven for feeling that he has been given the ultimate accolade.

Mr Bird is pleased about the compliment, but worried. He spends most of his life in a tizz about some-

Dickie Bird

thing or other. It would, of course, be perfectly natural for anyone to worry about living up to a reputation of being the best in the world at a particular job. And if this was all he had to be concerned about, Mr Bird would be a happy man.

However, he is adept at inventing worry. He will, for instance, worry about getting to Heathrow to catch his flight to the West Indies on time. Having arrived at the airport, he will worry about the pilot being able to find the West Indies. When he is in the air he will worry about whether he left the gas on at home in Barnsley. You think I exaggerate?

This is the man who went to his doctor for an inoculation and ended up having a cystoscopy. Even he cannot fathom how a single jab against typhoid and yellow fever turned into an examination of his prostate. 'I worry about everything. I even worry about the odd time I'm not worried. I think something must be wrong. I'm one of nature's witterers,' he says.

I have known him for forty years and he could have wittered for England when he was a teenager. He used to sit in the pavilion at Barnsley and chew his fingernails through his batting gloves while waiting for his turn at the wicket. On one occasion, and God knows how, he managed to fasten his batting pads together at the knees so that when it came to the moment he had to stride to the wickets he stood up and fell flat on his face.

Invited to lunch with the Queen at Buckingham Palace, he turned up at half-past eight in the morning. 'What's happening, Dickie?' the policeman asked.

'I've come for lunch with Her Majesty,' explained her most loyal subject.

'You're a bit early for that,' said the law. 'We can't let you in until after the Changing of the Guard.'

'What should I do?' said the world's greatest umpire, beginning to worry.

'Find a café and have a cup of coffee,' the policeman suggested.

'But tha' reckons I've got four hours to kill,' said the Queen's lunch guest.

'Have two cups of coffee,' said the bobby.

Having a private lunch with Her Majesty was a great moment in Mr Bird's life and when he describes what happens you have to imagine his manner of delivery. When he is telling a favourite anecdote Mr Bird stands up. When he does so he sometimes knocks over the furniture in his attempt to get at the story. He delivers in a loud, clear voice while looking over his shoulder, worrying in case someone might report him to the management.

'Somebody told me, "Dickie, when tha' dines with the Queen don't eat t'grapes. Tha' sees, they give you these great big scissors to cut them with and if tha's not used to 'em tha' could have a disaster on thi' hands." Well, I wished he hadn't told me because I wittered about them grapes all week. Anyway, when the time came I was in a terrible state and instead of refusing them I said I'd like some. Well, they gave me these long scissors and when I tried to cut t'grapes they shot all over t'room. They flew past the Queen and went all over the floor.'

At this point Dickie Bird's face is suffused with worry as if spattering the monarch with grapes was a treasonable offence. 'What happened?' I asked.

'Well, the Queen just looked at me and said, "Don't worry, Dickie, the corgis will take care of things." And does tha' know t'corgis ran in t'room and ate t'lot!' He paused. 'Must happen all t'time,' he said, hopefully.

I wondered if he was nervous before a game. 'Terrible,' he said. 'In and out of the toilet. Can't stop wittering. But once I'm on the field I change. I become calm and focused. I'm never thrown by what happens out there.' Ashley Harvey-Walker, the former Derbyshire player, once handed Dickie his false teeth on a pig of a wicket at Buxton. Dickie enquired whom he should give them to in the event of Mr Harvey-Walker not surviving the over.

There have, however, been moments when he has been fazed. There was that time during a Test match when Allan Lamb walked in to bat and handed Dickie his portable phone. 'What's this?' said Dickie. 'A phone,' said Allan Lamb. 'And what does tha' expect me to do wi' it?' asked the umpire. 'Take calls,' said the player.

The prospect of a phone ringing in his pocket during a Test match triggered a few of Dickie's worry symptoms: the ruminative rub of the jaw, the shooting out of his arms in front of him in the manner of his great hero Tommy Cooper, 'Just like that, ahem.' The phone rang. 'Umpire Bird here,' said Dickie. 'Tell that bloody man Lamb to get a move on,' said Ian Botham.

Lamb has often been Bird's nemesis. At Old Trafford

he removed all the wheels from the umpire's car and left it standing on bricks. On another occasion he locked the umpire's room from the outside and led his team on to the field, leaving Dickie Bird and his fellow official imprisoned. Play was held up while a steward found a sledgehammer big enough to knock the door down, by which time Dickie Bird was a gibbering wreck.

I dwell on these anecdotes because he loves telling them and they give an insight into his formidable sense of humour. The man you see on television, the twitchy, careworn, fraught individual with head bowed against the troubles of the world, is only a part of the whole being. There is a lot of laughter in him. His cap is homage to Albert Modley, an old-time northern music-hall comedian. He adores Tommy Cooper and Benny Hill. When he has a good laugh, like we did the other day, he sometimes cries with joy.

When Garfield Sobers appeared on Dickie's *This Is Your Life*, the umpire shed tears of happiness. 'Oh, master,' he said to Sobers. In all his years in the game, both as player and umpire, he has never lost his love for cricket's artistes.

Who have been the players to move him to tears? Well, Sobers apart, there's Lillee – 'the greatest, that's all you can say – the best'; Barry and Viv Richards; Boycott and Border – 'I'd have those two batting for my life any day'; Graeme Pollock, Greg Chappell, Michael Holding, Richard Hadlee. There are more.

'Fastest bowler I ever saw through the air was Frank Tyson. Lightning. Bowled against me at Scarborough

and I went on the front foot and hit the first three balls through midwicket for four.

'As he bowled the fourth I was again on the front and all I remember was hearing him say, "Hit that bugger for four." Next thing I heard was the ambulance they sent to take me to hospital. I was trying to get up, saying, "Wheer's that Tyson? I'll reighten him if I get hold of him!"' He points to a dent in his jawline. 'Still feel it when it's cold,' he said.

He feels Wasim Akram, Waqar Younis, Curtly Ambrose and Malcolm Marshall are as good as any he has seen; Les Jackson comes close. 'Two Tests for England, it's a joke. If he played nowadays he'd be automatic choice. Played against him once and he kept hitting me in t'rib cage. I went down t'wicket and said, "I wish tha'd stop bowling like that," and he said, "Why?" And I said, "Because I'm not good enough to hit thi' that's why."'

He is not keen on a third umpire and electronic assistance. Reckons it takes something away from the craft of being an umpire. 'Also, it slows the game down. In any case, controversy is part of the game. I've always found players are understanding, provided you treat them right. They used to say Ian Chappell was a handful. Never had a problem. Lovely guy, marvellous cricketer. That Merv Hughes, he's a beauty,' he said. I asked him about sledging. 'Not a problem,' he said. I suspect they dare not try it on in his company. Neutral umpires? 'All right, provided they are the best fourteen or so in the world and not selected on a quota basis.'

He will be sixty later this month and he lives alone. When he recently confessed to a television interviewer that he was sometimes lonely he received several offers of marriage, but he has already worked that one out. 'Nearly been married twice, but it wouldn't be fair with all the travelling I do. In any case, I'm married to cricket,' he said. If anyone else said that it would sound daft. Coming from Dickie Bird you accept it as a fair summation of his life.

When I asked him what gave him most satisfaction in life he said he thought it was that his fellow professionals 'trusted' him. Interesting choice of word; not 'loved him' or 'admired him' but gave him their 'trust'. When we parted I wished him well in the West Indies but I knew we would speak again before he left.

Sure enough I had been home five minutes when he called. He was worried in case I had misunderstood one or two of the things he had said. He told me he had been awake all night replaying our evening in his mind.

We checked the areas of his concern: fifty-three Tests, eighty-two one-day internationals, four World Cups, not to mention meeting the Queen and Lady Thatcher and John Major; not bad for a Barnsley lad.

'It was great the other night. It's been a long time since I laughed like that,' he said. He sounded worried.

April 1993

O<small>N</small> Thursday Lord's was a special place to be. It always is, but Dickie Bird's farewell provided another reason for being there. The night before, I called and asked how he felt. 'Like Marilyn Monroe,' he said. His Test match career might have ended but the build-up to his final retirement next season is only just beginning. It seems everyone wants a piece of Dickie Bird. The intensive media interest leading up to and beyond the tearful walk to the wicket did much to demonstrate how he has been transformed from a cricket character to a national treasure. He should be taken over by the Heritage Department immediately.

Two recent books pinpoint his lovable eccentricity. Brian Scovell's collection of tributes to Dickie contains a reminder of the way he introduces himself to people. He was once sunning himself in my back garden when the window cleaner came round the corner. Dickie jumped to his feet and rushed over to the man. 'Good morning, I'm Dickie Bird, Test match umpire,' he said. According to the book, he did the same thing when swimming in Barbados alongside a very large bather. 'I'm Dickie Bird, Test match umpire,' he said. The large man looked bemused. 'I'm Luciano Pavarotti,' he said. Not for the first time in his life, Mr Bird was flummoxed.

June 1996

D<small>ICKIE</small> B<small>IRD</small> umpired his last game of county cricket yesterday. Missing him already, as the

Americans say. In the past thirty years or more he has become the most unlikely icon produced by any game. He is a rum mixture, a man who is naturally funny and yet instinctively pessimistic, someone who is by nature friendly yet who chooses a lonely life. As an umpire, he brought a natural authority to the most difficult of jobs, yet he is flummoxed by the thought of boiling an egg and sometimes needs a map to find his way out of a car park.

In fact, anything not to do with cricket baffles him. They've got to find him something to do otherwise he will haunt the game like a forlorn ghost. Let him advise and supervise international umpires. On the evidence of the summer one or two require help. He doesn't need the money. Apart from the fact he has never spent very much, he made a bob or two out of his autobiography. On the strength of the book's success he is buying a new car and thinking of a holiday. Where? Australia. Where else?

To date the book has sold 350,000 copies in hardback. Messrs Hoddle and Adams eat your hearts out. Dickie Bird's story is not about sleaze and scandal or dressing-room tittle-tattle. Instead it's an account of a love affair between a man and a game. Corny and old-fashioned? Maybe. But it is also a reminder of the real reason we all watch or play, why we are all capable of being made lovelorn and foolish by a silly game.

You have earned your retirement, old mate. Take it easy. Relax. Fat chance.

September 1998

There are few cricket functions in Yorkshire to which Dickie Bird is not invited and few he does not attend. His appetite for the game is undiminished and he is president of countless societies. He has had a suite and a clock named after him in the new East Stand at Headingley, and continues to be a best-selling author.